THE RIVER WITHIN

by

Karen Rose Schultz

Inner Space Publishing
900 Jorie Blvd., Suite 234
Oak Brook, IL 60521

First printing 1993

ISBN 0-9636082-5-8

LCCN 93-77831

Dedication

This book is dedicated to recovering people everywhere. It is especially dedicated to incest survivors and those who have the courage to recover from a terror-filled childhood. Keep your hope! Be aware of and tap into your inner strength and power. Believe in the love and the light that is inside you.

Acknowledgments

Appreciation is expressed to the following individuals for their support, help, sharing, and belief in this book:

To Richard S. Schultz, my husband, whose faith and belief in me is a valued and treasured gift. His support has enabled me to reach for the stars and have my feet planted on the ground at the same time! Thanks for encouraging me to be the best I can be. Your computer knowledge was a Godsend!

To Sara May, a dear friend who gave me wonderful feedback on the book! Thanks.

To Virginia McCullough who edited the book. Her input and suggestions helped energize me to complete this book.

To Mr. Wayne Vanek, a wonderful and special person who has helped me greatly in the area of self-discovery and growth.

To the Sunday Night ACOA group. You all have been terrific motivators and friends. Your enthusiasm for the book gave me a sense of purpose and meaning.

To all of my clients, past and present. To all workshop participants—your input was greatly appreciated. You have all taught me more than you will ever know.

To Sue Havertine, a dear friend who is an inspiration and a beautiful person. Her support and encouragement continue to be an invaluable resource.

To Nadine Grant, a terrific teacher, speaker, and mentor. Your help made this book and my speaking career possible and memorable.

To Bernie Dugan, my supervisor. Thanks for your support and guidance.

To my mother, Laura. Thanks for showing me that people do not give up despite obstacles, illness, lack of finances, and opportunities. This book is the "open door" you always told me about!

To Eleanore Feldman, who offered me a safe place to ask for help. Your group helped me to write this book. You are a special person. Thanks for being there.

To Kathleen Wright, Donna Bielby, Jenna Eisenberg, and Dr. Steve Humowlecki. Your care and concern about my physical and emotional health through yoga, massage, chiropractic adjustments, and medical care have helped me greatly. You are all valued and vital to my life. Thanks for your efforts on my behalf.

To Kevin Dubrow, who believed in me when I didn't believe in myself. Thank you for your support, caring, and interest in my growth.

Table of Contents

The River Within

She looks in the mirror
And feels the coolness

It soothes her, and holds her
Inside.

The air is crisp, the path is clear,
as the river flows in and out of the mossy flatland.

She cries out,
and lets the river wash away the tears.

She is thirsty,
and so she sips the water.

As her life gets filled,
she knows she must share the river

with others who are dear to her.
The river that flows constantly is

The self.
That draws strength from the seasons.

Like life, the river will rise and fall.
And there she will always remain,

Standing proud and tall.

Introduction

As a child, I used to sit in my room and talk into a tape recorder. My voice was something I cherished even then. I found comfort in playing my voice back to me, validating that I was truly alive. Never sharing my true feelings with anyone, I spent most of my childhood isolated. People in junior high and high school would always come up to me and tell me their secrets as if I was a counselor or therapist. This was great! I could get paid for this! I became a social worker not only to build on my gift, but to "fix" my family.

I thought if I fixed them, I'd be healthy. In reality, there were a few secrets I was sure to take with me to the grave. I would numb my feelings and pretend all was well. I often hid in my silence and intellect, believing I was powerful and all-knowing. It was always others who needed help. Later on, I hid in my social work training and pretended to be healthy.

In reality, I suffered from several eating disorders: bulimia, anorexia, and compulsive overeating. I switched back and forth between them, always going to extremes and harming myself. By picking abusive men and becoming codependent, I gained my identity, approval, and validation from these men. Believing I was super talented and better than everyone else, I switched addictions after graduate school and became a workaholic.

In truth, I couldn't fix my family and realized my attempt to get revenge for my anger toward them only hurt me. I felt inadequate, inferior, and could not express my anger at home. Being a perfectionist, it was always all or nothing. I wouldn't allow myself to make mistakes and risk failure, so I'd never take any risks. I'd then beat myself up with all of my self-hate and negative, abusive self-talk. "You are stupid," and "you are a loser," I would say to myself, becoming my own worst enemy. When imprisoned in my private hell, I used a smile as a mask to cover up the truth of how wounded and shame-filled I really felt.

I grew up in a dysfunctional family filled with alcoholism, divorce, abuse, violence, pain, and terror. I was finally able to heal and get the best revenge possible—learning to love myself and living a happy, healthy life. Finally able to see I didn't deserve self-abuse or punishment for sins and crimes I didn't commit, I forgave myself and learned to repair myself with positive messages and thoughts. The only person I could fix was me. *The River Within* is a testimony to my struggle to escape the bondage of a dysfunctional system and self-hatred.

By learning how to believe in my abilities, a 12-step program, therapy, and spirituality, I saved myself. My sense of spirituality came from adopting a lifestyle based on truth, honesty, and a belief in a power greater than myself. The idea of a higher power in a spiritual sense is different from the religious notion of God. The spiritual way of living encompasses a more direct relationship or partnership with God or a higher power.

A higher power can be a man, a woman, nature, or simply a universal energy. Most of us grew up thinking of God as an authority figure or a man with a white beard on a throne waiting to punish us for our sins. A spiritual relationship with God broadens this narrow view. It offers a more creative and loving image of God.

The major distinction in a spiritual lifestyle is the belief that a higher power or concept of God creates rather than destroys. The higher power is all loving and compassionate like a father or mother who loves unconditionally and doesn't punish or criticize a person who sins or makes mistakes. With this concept, we can move closer to our higher power and see him or her as a positive force in our lives. Our sense of higher power helps us to grow and does not exert power and control over our lives if we don't follow his or her commands. We choose to give our will and our lives to the care of our higher power as we understand him or her.

I now believe I can truly live my life, not just merely survive. Many miracles have occurred in my life and I will show you how to claim some miracles of your own. Are you just surviving, or are you finding meaning and purpose in your life? Are your negative thoughts and self-talk helping or harming you? I want you to know that whatever your background, you too can heal, thrive, and prosper.

The River Within is a powerful, positive, and lighted place located within you. This is your own resource and storehouse for love, acceptance, and self-esteem. A friend once told me, "All the answers are inside you." I didn't believe him. I'd always looked to others for my identity and validation. Believing in The River Within will help you, as it has me, to learn to trust yourself, reclaim your self-esteem, and empower you toward your greatest potential as a human being.

I didn't want to look within myself for fear of what I'd find there. Not wanting to deal with the hurt and pain, I pretended to be someone else—anyone else. I wanted to heal without grieving or expressing my pain. Marcel Proust reminds us, "We don't receive wisdom, we must discover it for ourselves after a journey that no one can take for us or spare us from."

Follow me into The River Within and be prepared to see the beauty and the love there. The good news is: you don't have to hide yourself in shame and guilt or feel as if you're a mistake, flawed or defective in some way. Have you ever thought there was something wrong with you? This is shame, the belief that you are a mistake. Remember when you hide your shame, you also hide the good inside as well.

When we come out of hiding, we can find the diamond that shines beneath our shame and pain. This book explains how we can create our own lives and change our lifescripts by breaking the rules. We can create the kind of life we want—rewrite the endings by breaking the rules of our childhood scripts. Changing our lifescripts is explored in all of my groups and workshops on spiritual growth and development.

When we tell our secrets to others in a safe place, we face the truth. Honesty and truth are the keys to spiritual growth. Telling these secrets frees us from having to hide the truth. I learned on the journey into The River Within that I didn't have to go anywhere or do anything to get help—I simply needed to ask a power greater than myself for help. This is recovery. Recovery helps you to forgive yourself, free your guilt and shame, and gives you tools to find a new way of life and new ways of coping. The recovery process also helps you to release and let go of all your addictions, distortions, and failures. This book explores recovery as it applies to happiness, intuition, and inner wisdom.

I've heard that people who are in recovery and a 12-step process are among the healthiest people around. Because the 12-step program gives us tools and a foundation for growth that our parents never taught us, we learn to live our lives to the fullest. We may have to go through our pain and not around it, but in the end we will live a lifestyle that positively influences our stress level, self-esteem, and view of others. Compassion for others and self-acceptance are the keys to self-love.

As a licensed clinical social worker in private practice, I work with adult children of dysfunctional families, depressed people, and those with eating disorders. While continuing in my own recovery program, I train other social workers to understand and use the 12-step program and teach people that spirituality is the bridge between addiction and recovery. I cheer them on as they take steps toward creating a balanced, healthy life. Spirituality is our birthright and is open to everyone.

I've been relentless in my search for a healthy life. No matter what your circumstances, you too can heal—starting now. I know the way to happiness and light and will be your guide on the journey to self-love. My passion comes from being violated and hurt. Knowing there had to be a better life out there, I was going to find it even if I had to crawl every step of the way. I found a way out of my private hell and know you can do the same.

My hypothesis is that people cannot recover and have a good sense of self-esteem if they continue to hide their true selves. People may think it is wrong to ask for help, so they try to change on their own. William Saroyan states, "Good people are good because they come to wisdom through failure."

I had to admit that I failed to solve my problems alone. The wisdom came when I attended my first 12-step meeting and realized I wasn't alone—other people were hurting as well. Mostly, serenity came by realizing I belonged. My clients have similar experiences when they take risks and attend a 12-step group meeting.

When I finally surrendered and admitted to needing help, I saved my life even though it felt like defeat. A person's pride and ego often get in the way of recovery; we must learn about humility and surrender to recover. To surrender is to be open to new ideas because all of your old coping mechanisms aren't working as they used to. When I finally admitted I was powerless, my life began to blossom.

One of the problems is we don't know or trust ourselves. Many of us trust others more easily than we trust ourselves. The answer is that to heal we must surrender to a power greater than ourselves. Before recovery, I was "playing God" or letting other people be my God or higher power. To heal I had to be humble and admit that as a human being there were limits to what I could truly do. I wasn't superhuman. To recover we must risk failure and risk being vulnerable while in a safe place. If we stifle, hide, or deny our true feelings, they come out in addictive or compulsive ways.

My workshops and groups help people get beyond pride and ego and focus on the positive and wise parts of themselves. I hope *The River Within* will do the same. Spirituality is defined as a way of life regarding self, others, nature, and what one believes to be beyond this world. Religion is an organized set of rules and traditions.

One may be spiritual but not have any ties to religion. Spiritual growth helps you become one whole person and creates connections, uniting all parts of a person into one cohesive whole. Many of us split off parts of ourselves we don't like, then criticize and judge others.

We need to have a better relationship with our true self and cross the bridge between addiction and recovery. We can go from wounded to wonderful—a workshop I facilitate. I'll be on the other side of the bridge, encouraging you to take the risk and try to cross over into recovery, offering you my hand as I reach out to steady you. Most importantly, you'll realize the power to get across was within you all the time.

1

Life's Unanswered Questions

Have you ever believed life will never get better, and you will have to live with your present circumstances forever? That's what I used to believe. For years I was so depressed and sad because of my family of origin. Just to escape from the truth of the pain of my childhood years, I used to wish I was adopted.

For years I lived with terrible secrets I refused to tell anyone about. Perhaps you've done the same out of shame and fear of acknowledging just how badly you were hurt. I found a way out of my private hell and can help you do the same. To offer hope to those of you who have suffered along the road from sickness to recovery, I'm writing this book.

It was so hard to admit to myself the family I'd been born into was not operating as a healthy system and that I was sick as a result of my family's dysfunction. I would numb my feelings and pretend all was well. To fix my family, I went to school to become a social worker. If I cured them, I thought, I'd be healthy. The sad reality was—the only person I could really heal was myself. As a social worker, I see in my clients so much of the same pain, fear, and frustration about their circumstances. I watch them go through the process of recovery—which is sometimes unbearable and excruciating for both of us. Why do I do it? Why have I chosen to deal with the pain and suffering of others?

I chose to help others with their pain because of the anger and outrage I feel and cannot understand or fully explain. For years I lived in my private hell and now have a burning desire to help others deal with their misery. I have so much passion about each person who chooses to embark on the road to health. For so long I felt impotent and powerless to change my life for the better. Facing each obstacle as if it was a dragon needing to be slain, I inched my way out of the hole I was in. I never gave up my hope and desire for a happy, healthy life.

I've climbed what seemed like mountains and have emerged as a victor on the other side of the pain to a beautiful, bright, and peaceful place. This place is my home. My purpose is to teach everyone how to find this inner sanctuary that allows each part of a person to be accepted and loved. This sanctuary is The River Within.

It is a safe, serene part of each of us that has all the resources we need. To gain access to this part of us, we need to learn to trust ourselves. We can focus on the positive, change old negative patterns, and ask for help from a power greater than ourselves. I believe everyone has a River Within. The River flows and is wise.

I like to think of a beautiful Queen inside me leading me to happiness. This Queen inside me guards the River and will be there with positive, gentle, and nurturing messages. The Queen is my higher self (or intuition) and knows what's best for me. To find The River Within and the Queen, or King, we must believe in our core of strength and call upon it when necessary. Why turn to drugs, alcohol, shopping, sex, or other addictions when the answers and the resources are inside you?

The reason I looked into The River Within is that for years I tried to rely on other people to satisfy my needs and to give me strength. I never took proper credit for my accomplishments. Many of my clients also do not give themselves the proper credit and respect they deserve. They don't have a feeling of self-worth. My clients and I have all faced obstacles and survived growing up in dysfunctional or imperfect families. We weren't taught to use the strength and the love inside ourselves.

We can create the kind of life we want if we connect the Queen or King inside us with a higher power. The higher power works with the King or Queen within and gives us loving guidance. Everyone can benefit from this relationship. If we allow the Queen (or King), our higher power, and our thoughts to focus on the positive, we can reach our potential as human beings.

My hairdresser recently asked me the difference between intuition and impulsive thinking. I told her that if you hear critical or negative messages and self-talk inside you, it's not your higher self speaking. This voice is the chatterbox and will lead you down old, familiar, yet negative paths. The higher self only speaks in a positive, gentle, and caring way. If the message asks you to be impulsive, this is not your intuition or higher self; intuition operates much slower and is calmer and more consistent.

The only way shame, codependent patterns, addictions, and depression can be legitimately healed is through a 12-step program. Also, in therapy we can examine self-defeating ways in which we have harmed ourselves as well as deal with feelings we may have denied or suppressed since childhood.

One thing my work has taught me is that many people are in pain and don't know what to do with it. We simply don't know how to share it, express it, or release it. We hold ourselves responsible for others' behavior and can't seem to forgive ourselves enough to let go of old resentments and fears. Until we allow ourselves to believe we have the power to express anger and resentment without killing anyone, we can't heal. We can love ourselves, turn shame into light, and explore the wealth and richness inside us.

A professional with many years of clinical experience behind me, I once attended a workshop on how to break into magazine writing. My desire was to create articles that shared both my strengths and struggles with childhood trauma and empowered people to rise above their circumstances and learn to love themselves. When the presenter asked us why we wanted to write, my reply was that I knew a lot about pain and loss and wanted to help others with their pain. No one spoke to me for the entire day except one man who wanted some job leads for his son who had just received his masters in social work. I even ate lunch alone because no one would approach me.

What I learned from that workshop, which, by the way, took place before I was aware of John Bradshaw and inner child material, was that people avoid their pain. We are a society in which people would rather laugh and reach for quick and impulsive solutions to their pain than look inward and face the pain. This is harder and much more dangerous than eating ice cream to mood alter or drown out their feelings.

Those of us who have the courage to look inward and examine our pain are free to use The River Within. Those who would prefer to distance, or distract, themselves from the pain will have addictions or compulsive habits. It is only when we feel the pain that it's released.

I have clients who've had traumatic childhoods, yet they never really connect the feeling of being abused with the memory of their childhood. Many of us are distant from the truth and don't see that the process of therapy helps us remember the event or events and allows us to feel the feelings associated with these events. Therapy also deals with grief and loss. After we feel the pain and grieve for our losses, we can let go of it and be free to fill that space with healthy coping skills. Many people have walls so thick they can't fathom taking them down, but I suggest these walls can be taken down slowly, or windows or doors put in first.

In therapy, history is important because the body does not forget trauma. The body holds the memories. I was so rigid in my body I felt bound and couldn't move freely. I held my tension in and never allowed myself to get a massage, thinking the touch would be somehow abusive or intrusive. However, from getting massages regularly, I learned the massage helped me to heal and to release the trauma and painful memories.

History is also important for looking at the attitudes, values, and beliefs a person is operating with. Once a therapist collects the data, a treatment plan is shared with the client. Not all therapeutic techniques can be used with everyone. With my clients, I try to give them what they need, not apply one treatment plan to everyone.

For example, if you've always heard that self-affirmation is conceited or selfish, the way you operate in the world will be affected. Many clients have a hard time patting themselves on the back or celebrating an accomplishment. Remember, it's not selfish to affirm or congratulate oneself for a job well done. Living by the old thinking patterns limits how much self-love and self-esteem can be built.

There is a connection between the body and the mind. If your parent or parents were rageaholics or if they fought regularly, your body would hold in those memories. For years, I separated my intellect from my emotions. I lived in my head and never experienced my feelings of exhaustion. I once had a broken toe and jogged eight miles a day for several weeks before my podiatrist told me a toe was broken.

This points out how profoundly I numbed, or dissociated, my body from the rest of me. Part of healing involves reconnecting the mind and the body. I may be upset if I feel my body being tired, but it's a lot better to know my limits and to admit I'm not a superwoman. This is healing in itself. Many people who come to therapy know they're tired or in pain, but they also know how to numb or ignore it.

Therapists try to help people get in touch with and start feeling the body and help them listen to what their body is saying. Therapists hook up the intellect with the emotions as well. An easier way to see the therapy process is to see it as a journey to the center of the earth or to the core self inside you. This core is beautiful but some people have trouble healing the shame protecting the core self—the true self.

Shame makes us believe we're a mistake, or flawed and defective in some way, and we want to hide. Shame makes us fear exposure because we feel if anyone saw the real person inside, they wouldn't like us. This stops us from getting close to anyone and we become isolated, lonely, and sad. However, underneath the shame is a part of us that is authentic, healthy, and genuine. We can unmask this true self and live a life of authenticity.

Yoga helps me to get in touch with feelings in my body, helps me to clear out the toxins inside me, and releases all the negative emotions I collect while working intensely with people in recovery. I then have space for growth, movement, or good feelings. Other healing techniques I have had wonderful success with include massage therapy and chiropractic adjustments. Just make sure you trust the person providing these services; get a referral from someone you trust.

Therapy operates in much the same way—by exposing the trauma or painful feelings in a safe place, working through it, and healing. The release of the negative, toxic material helps create space for light, love, and positive self-esteem. We need to be on our own healing journey before we can help others with their pain.

Although it took a long time to undo the effects of the first eighteen years of my life, I found a way to crawl and then walk out of my denial and pain into a happy life. I know every pitfall and every nook and cranny of self-hatred and self-abuse. Long before I tried to heal myself, I tried to annihilate myself. I know every trick and every rationalization others use to stop themselves from releasing the hurt and the pain. I know what it's like to be in codependent relationships that drained me of my self-esteem and power because I gave the power to others I thought could be the good parents I never had. And lastly, I know how to blame and give away all of my goodness and kindness to others while neglecting and hating myself.

If you add up all the events and traumas in my life, you'd be amazed how I was able to overcome as much as I did. Think about the obstacles you have overcome. You can read this book and get in touch with yourself without being me or imitating my recovery process. You can start now and get as far as I am and beyond. We all have the capacity to embrace ourselves and live a spiritual life. My story is similar to others' stories of horror, pain, abuse, and fear. My higher self has asked me to bring this message of hope to you. Whatever your story is, you can heal.

Who Had the Worst Childhood?

I was so proud of the way in which I viewed my childhood. I couldn't believe anyone had a childhood as harmful and traumatic as mine. Incest, mental illness, physical, ritualistic and emotional abuse, and alcoholism were all issues I had to deal with. Because I was so different and thought others wouldn't understand, I never wanted to share the pain and the truth with anyone. I thought I was unique, and developed a false sense of self-esteem. Colleagues who knew me remarked I was the most courageous person they knew. Not only was that not true, I realized by thinking this I had closed myself off to any meaningful friendship or sharing.

As a social worker, I wasn't prone to attending a 12-step or self-help group. "I refer people there," I thought, "I don't need that." However, the truth was I felt very lonely and sad, but maintained the idea that I was strong and needed no love. On trips to the institutions my mother went in and out of as a child, I'd stand like a soldier going into battle. I never cried or showed any emotion.

There were so many nights and days I lived in fear, yet I never let anyone see me crying or exhausted. This struggle to hide my true feelings has taken much out of me. I hid my true self inside a darkness that never saw the light. I cried alone and refused to hear anyone else's story for fear I'd break down. By going to Adult Children of Alcoholics (ACOA), I realized we were all hurt and abused and that my story was not as terrible as the stories of others. My story is important only as a guide. Take what you want and leave the rest. If I can help just one person figure something out or offer hope to others struggling with recovery, then this book will have served its purpose.

I was torn between wanting to write this book to get back at my father or because I believed in my message and in myself. All my life I've struggled with this conflict. Perhaps the rage and hurt I feel toward my father could be resolved if I knew more about his childhood. It would help me understand his pain and I'm sure I would then be able to have some compassion for him. This is only because I've gone through the anger, depression, denial, loss, and the fantasy of thinking we could put the past to rest. I realized this would never happen.

Even when I never saw my father, I felt bonded to him. John Bradshaw calls this "traumatic bonding." Bonding to the abuser is not healthy. In therapy, I try to help others distance from and break this inappropriate bond. If you've been abused and feel drawn to your abuser, you're not crazy. Children want a father or mother so badly they keep going back to that parent hoping someday he or she will be the type of parent the child needs. I would urge anyone dealing with father issues to heal yourself. After spending many years looking for father substitutes and praying for a reconciliation, I realized the only person I could reconcile with was myself.

Another reason I wanted to write this book is to serve others. I want to give to all of you the gifts and knowledge I've been fortunate enough to learn on the recovery road. This road is easy to find but not easy to follow. How many of us choose this road over addiction and self-abuse? Those with the desire and the fortitude to walk this road will be rewarded one hundred times over. Those who never find the road are unfortunate.

The road will appear if you ask for it to appear. Anyone can ask God directions and he will open your heart enough for you to get there. My purpose is to be your guide to this road. The rest of the journey is up to you. Do you want to reach your potential as a human being? Do you want to be happy and successful as a person? Then follow me into The River Within.

The River Within flows and gives you all the knowledge you need. Throughout this book we will be exploring The River Within. I want every one of you to hang in there, because there is a way out and I can show it to you. What took me years of searching to find I will entrust to you, and pray that your struggle can continue on a more structured and clear path.

How Can We Heal?

I was driven to succeed by my anger and rage, even when I paid the psychological and physical costs of using rage for motivation. My health and sense of security were jeopardized because I often turned this anger and rage against myself. Maybe I needed to be propelled by my anger and rage in the beginning, but I kept using that coping mechanism long after its effectiveness had worn off.

Many clients come to therapy with the same problem. Their old coping mechanisms don't work in the present and are now destructive to the person's well-being. Therapy also involves changing those patterns and putting in new ways to function. Picture a new road or a new house being built. The old foundation needs to be taken out and a new one put in its place. This new foundation can be a 12-step program. The program a creates a new, functional foundation so people can thrive and prosper.

Without my relationship to the divine aspect inside me, I could never have gone through the obstacles and the fear to reach my true self. I could never have found my self-esteem or learned to trust myself without that new foundation. How many of you have no idea who you are? How many of you believe you have no self or identity apart from your parents? Let me assure you that you have a self inside. You just need to get to know yourself better. All the stories about aliens and intruders from outer space make me laugh. Do you know that many of us are alien to ourselves? We wonder where parts of us come from and we don't believe in our own capacity to know and love ourselves.

My inner self is like my best friend. For years I tried to find best friends everywhere but inside myself. Before you worry about aliens from space, start looking for the stranger or alien inside of you. The better you know yourself, the more whole, cohesive, and happy you become. Life is a journey into the center of your own self; a journey filled with opportunity, chances to grow, and a new foundation. You need to believe you can reach your potential as a human being.

As a social worker in private practice, I deal mostly with people wanting to find out what's causing their present pain and concerns. For example, many adult children of alcoholics come to me because they keep picking alcoholic or needy partners and wind up being dumped, dropped, mistreated, or all the above. Many are not in touch with their self-sabotage and lack of self-worth and deserving. They're addicted to other people because they don't know who they are. This is called codependency and it is a killer. According to John Bradshaw, it's the most common family illness. He calls codependency "spiritual bankruptcy."

Living a codependent life sucks all the self-esteem and spirituality out of you until the life inside you is gone. Why do people choose this? My answer as a professional is that they learned it as a child because they had no choice. We are often taught that looking good and approving of ourselves is selfish. We shy away from applauding ourselves and look for approval and validation from others. This can lead to allowing others to define, judge, and manipulate us.

Codependents give and give hoping to receive, but never get a return on their investment. We need to invest more in our own lives. How much time do you spend focused on other's lives instead of your own? We need to have a better relationship with ourselves and with a power greater than us—the only force that can really be our ultimate parent and guardian.

Everyone who has ever been abused, harmed, or mistreated asks me to explain why God lets violent and traumatic events happen. I was one of those people so angry at God that I strayed far away from him. For most of my adult life people tried to bring me a message from God, but I wouldn't listen.

My only contact with God during these years was to light a candle when I felt I had no reason to live and wanted to die. I'd almost given up on life but I had a spark of hope I would not relinquish. At the time, I didn't know where this spark came from but I now realize the light was inside me. Lighting the candle only validated that I continued to have a bit of hope about my life. Is there a spark of hope left inside you? You need this spark to understand the spiritual process. Even if you're not in touch with the light inside you, I want you to know it's there.

I was hurt that God wasn't more active in helping me out of my despair. Another question this book addresses is "How can we return to God and work through our anger and hurt enough to reconnect and reestablish communication with him?" I say "him" because that's how I define my higher power, or God. You may have another way to address your idea of a higher power and that's fine.

The 12-step program of Adult Children of Alcoholics has been a tremendous force in this regard. Just what is the 12-step program? The concepts and program issues will be discussed and made simple. Even though you can't *see* how it works, I'll help you make sense out of the spiritual process. You might be thinking, 'How can I believe and have faith in a process if I can't see how it works?' Since faith has so much to do with the program, this question is explored. The program concepts and ideas will be introduced through personal stories, program literature, and fairy tales I have written.

This program has worked for millions of people and it is truly the only way I have found to help a recovering person come back to life. Coupled with therapy, this program has led to much healing—not only for me but for my clients as well. When we have a wake-up call, we realize we're not sure just how much time we have to live. If not now, when will we decide to face the fear and roam into the unknown?

Concept of a Higher Power or God

Throughout the book, it's important for you to define and feel comfortable with your own view of God or a higher power. A person's definition of God is not as important as how he or she relates to and understands God.

Just remember I'm not trying to say one concept is better or worse. I'm only telling you the way I was raised, and using spirituality as an alternative to thinking about God in a traditional sense. My husband, a devout Catholic, attends church daily. We go to church as a couple, and even though I'm spiritual in nature, rather than traditionally religious, we still accept and understand each other's concepts.

Many times dysfunctional families use God to reinforce their beliefs and practices. For example, God's power is often introduced to reinforce punishment for wrongdoing. Hence, a child may really fear his or her parents, and God is often thrown in to make the child fear punishment from two sources (heaven and earth). This is the way most of my clients have experienced God in their upbringing.

The Therapy Process Made Simple

The therapy process is much like the 12-step process. I try to build a foundation and a structure for clients who don't have one. When you grow up in a dysfunctional home as I did, you soon realize there is nothing to build on to create a positive self-concept or self-esteem. Negative thoughts and ideas permeate the mind and become internalized. The emotional component of nurturing, positive mirroring, and an environment built from trust and security is rarely seen. In therapy I create an environment for each person so they can grow, believe in their strengths, and be aware of the negative tapes they might have heard as a child (the chatterbox). Emotions such as shame, guilt, and fear are also discussed.

How can *you* also be an inspiration to others? By practicing the principles outlined here, you can become your own champion and gain inspiration. My goal is not to inflate my ego to star status but to let you know that I've overcome many obstacles and continue on the journey toward self-acceptance.

Are you saying to yourself, "See, she did it, and I haven't"? Don't judge yourself for not having what it takes to be where I am in my life. I will empower you! My goal is not to make you feel less about yourself—it's to help you get across the bridge between addiction and recovery. To accomplish this, I'm going to show you both my strengths and my weaknesses. I'm not strong in every area of my life; I still have to fight self-abuse and negative self-talk on a daily basis. Even so, I was able to grow and prosper in many areas—you can too.

Anyone with the courage and the fortitude to embark on the journey to recovery is an inspiration. My story is only one of many, and I'm proud of my accomplishments. However, I'm not trying to hold myself up as a perfect being. Give yourself permission to do the same.

Love yourself and accept your limitations. At first I wasn't able to because it was too painful. Now it's getting a little easier. Think about how hard you are on yourself. Embrace your accomplishments and feel proud of yourself. For years I didn't and allowed others to hold esteemed positions in my life. I had to be proud of myself and not give others the admiration and praise I needed for my own self-esteem to grow.

The River Within also offers you expert advice from the therapist part of me. I have worked many years in the social work field in a teaching and training capacity as well as leading my own workshops and groups. As such, I've learned some valuable information about building self-esteem and I want to help you grow as my clients have grown.

A man from a 12-step program sat next to me at a professional speakers' meeting recently. I told him I was in a recovery process. He said his work and his program had never intersected on any level before. This surprised me. My work and my recovery program have indeed intersected. It's hard to separate me totally from my work. I tried this before and never made connections to others. I merely hid myself and attempted to imitate others I thought were more gifted. Constantly in my role as a therapist, I sounded very stiff. I like myself better when I speak from the heart and not from any intellectual framework.

2

Victimization and the Cast of Characters

I have a life as a victim and a life as a survivor. The difference between the two is amazing. I'm sharing this to illustrate how locating and tapping into The River Within and a 12-step program changed my life. What happens between these two extremes is the most important point in this book. As you are going through this chapter, try to focus on the victim part of me and note how I was transformed into a loving, healthy, and thriving human being. This transformation is available to you even if you've never been victimized and severely abused.

My history is important because it weaves a story and a fabric that's unique. Just like a needlepoint picture, you get to see what events shaped my life. You can see the interconnections, the mistakes, the beauty, and the triumphs. My history also explains that I chose to reconnect with most of my family of origin. I had to make a choice about my father and chose not to continue my efforts to reconnect with him. I wanted to break the cycle of abuse in my family—to be the one who would shine and the one who could have a healthy family and life.

Chains of bondage are hard to break. The only way out of a cave or a self-made prison is to deal with your own anger and hurt. The hardest part is to believe you don't have to live a "dead" life just because you were betrayed, used, or tortured. My recovery involves learning more about myself as well as reconnecting all the fragments and splintered parts of myself that I have a hard time claiming. I can reclaim my life if I choose to.

My father has a picture on his wall of me as a baby. He will not give me back this picture. In the picture, I'm three years old—cute, smiling, and innocent. I want that little girl back. He thinks he still owns my inner child if he doesn't give me the picture. He's greatly mistaken. My inner child lives in me and is loved, honored, and cherished. This is what victims need to do after dealing with the anger and devastation they felt as children or teenagers. The best revenge is to search for wholeness, love, and beauty—to have a happy, healthy life. I'll take all the rage and pain inflicted on me and turn it inside out into loving and caring about myself and the world.

My family could not provide the motivation, the resources, or the support I needed. All the support and love had to come from inside me, with help from therapists and my higher power. Those of you who feel alone as you embark on a healing process can find support as well.

Those who are survivors often face fear and don't know if they're crazy or making it up. Believe in your intuition. A deep part of you knows the truth. Many of my clients are intimidated by family members who minimize, deny, or conveniently forget the truth they know. I hear them and believe them. This is something

I needed from others and didn't receive. You aren't bad, although bad things were done to you. The hardest feeling to deal with was the guilt that maybe I'd done something to deserve the abuse. We all deserve love and compassion.

Being victimized destroys any trust you have in the world. I urge you to find a safe place to talk about your feelings. Learn from other survivors and attend any meeting that can offer you strength, hope, and a healing touch. Being a victim doesn't have to destroy your life. Many clients work with me and their memories are sometimes vague and confusing. The more we can speak out the less we're controlled by old messages of defeatism and powerlessness.

To heal any wounds from an abusive or traumatic past is to know, accept, and feel the reality of what actually happened. I joined an incest survivor's group in 1990 and stayed in the group for eight months, expressing shameful feelings, connecting the memories with feelings, and sharing my pain with others who have also suffered and survived. What I found was a sense of power which helped me to grow and to risk talking about the parts of me that were stuck in shame and despair. I let all of my defenses down and wept.

The group was the best investment I've ever made. As a result of being in this group I started writing the story of my life. Although the story tumbled out of my gut in a random pattern, I was able to put all the pieces together. Just being able to write it down increased my energy and helped turn years of guilt and shame into purpose and power.

Victimization is a hard word to define. Many can't seem to comprehend that if we were hurt as children, we should avoid getting hurt in the future. Haven't we learned our lesson? A man at one of my ACOA groups asked, "Why do women want to be abused by unhealthy men?" "Because we were all abused," I replied. I know it isn't as simple as I'm making it but have you ever heard of a concept called imprinting? Imprinting has to do with repeating the negative and abusive patterns you learned as a child. It's in my brain and in my thoughts that I'm a victim. Codependency is also a learned behavior.

Any opportunity to become a victim feels like home to me. I know what it feels like, so I'm drawn to it. When I constantly heard my father being a critical, demeaning, and rude man, I thought all men were like that. I'd pick a mate based on what was familiar and known. I could pick out an alcoholic in a crowd. I'd go up to these men and try to start a relationship. Of course, I would end up being hurt, demoralized, and drained.

If I hadn't been in therapy to understand why I kept wanting to hurt myself, I'd have continued to follow this pattern. Survivors do not easily become willing to let go of the old, familiar ways. We need to let them know they're entitled to a happy and healthy life.

I've heard countless social workers say it frustrates them that some women stay in marriages like prison cells. Why can't they leave? The answer is they don't believe they have the option to leave an unhealthy or abusive person. These women feel trapped, empty, lost, and mostly invisible. Why do I get tired of abusing myself—only to give that power to a man? I don't think I have value or worth. This is what my victim part says. The good news is I can choose not to become a victim as an adult. I can recognize and identify the feelings and thoughts that lead me to believe there are no options. I can heal, change, and grow.

This is the therapy process and I've been able to help many survivors in this way. Usually there's a part of the survivors that leads them to be hurt and this part must be embraced so it can grow and be reparented. This is what I do with my clients. Most of the time this part operates unconsciously, which makes it hard to identify.

My own therapy has been diverse and varied. I've learned a tremendous amount from all of my prior therapists, men and woman alike. Without these experiences, I wouldn't be where I am today. That's because I went out and found the help I needed. You too can do this as part of your healing process.

I'm grateful to have worked with some of my former therapists. However, there was one technique which helped me deal specifically with the victimized parts of me. I'm sharing this process with you only as an illustration. Don't attempt to embark on cast of character work without the advice or consent from a therapist or qualified professional. If you are mentally ill or suffer from multiple personality disorder, continue with caution. If you become overwhelmed by or if you are uncomfortable with victimization issues, please go on to the next chapter.

Cast of Characters

During my therapy process I was able to separate parts of myself by using a technique entitled "cast of characters." My therapist urged me to write down what "characters" were inside me. If I gave each part a name, I would no longer split off the parts I didn't want. At first I thought my therapist was saying I was Sybil or something. However, the exercise was just a way for us to talk about the parts of me that operated in the world. I was also instructed to put down what age I believed each character was. I had Sheila, an adult; Marie, sixteen; Jeff (who is really Jennifer), twelve; Eugenia, five; and, Mary, one year old. I had other characters at different times but these were the most verbal.

Sheila: Queen of Control

Sheila is my "false self" persona. She gets me through the day. She is all intellect. She pretends to be happy and "fronts" for the other characters. She can be assertive and can make good decisions but is exhausted and feels overwhelmed. Sheila doesn't tell anyone how she really feels or know how to ask for help. She's proud and confident even when she doesn't actually feel that way. Many times Sheila has been the one to carry on, even with a terrible self-image. Sheila hates fun and emotion. She's like a machine in her approach to the world.

I first found out about Sheila while writing a story for a contest. The story was about a divorced woman who was able to get therapy and move on with her life. The character was a composite of all the women I'd ever worked with. The main character went to see a therapist named Sheila. The story, "Shelter in the Forest," was submitted to *New Woman* magazine. Although I lost the contest, I gained some good insight into myself. I sent the story to an editor in California who had read some of my stories and she thought the story was my own story. It was similar to my mother's story about her divorce and was from my clinical experience.

I was very frightened and felt vulnerable and exposed. When I thought the editor knew the real me, I wrote her back on professional stationery. She was very surprised, as she was convinced the main character was me. Years later, I realized I did have a part of my mother inside me, although I wasn't yet ready to accept it. The story continued after the main character left the therapist's office. I started writing about Sheila and how lost and depressed she felt.

I learned she didn't like being a therapist because she always had to appear to be very strong. Also, I learned Sheila wanted to be a writer, not a social worker. She wanted to cry, to be weak sometimes, and was lonely and sad.

During my young adulthood Sheila was very rigid in her approach to life. The different parts had different agendas and Sheila was asked to provide energy and to be responsible. She made some very poor choices in college and often had to succeed and fail at the same time.

Sheila had to hide the true part of herself. The only time she ever showed any emotion in college was when her boyfriend broke up with her. Sheila wound up in the school psychiatrist's office and told the story of her childhood. The psychiatrist couldn't believe she had come out of her family system intact. He said, "I'm surprised to see you here." Even though Sheila was accepted at one of the best state schools in upstate New York, she felt unworthy and thought she was a fake. It was Sheila's job to fool everyone about her past.

During college, Sheila had to prove to everyone she was competent and in control. Even her boyfriend didn't know the pain and torment she felt. Sheila started vomiting or restricting her food intake after she had her first sexual experience at the age of eighteen. The abuse issues came back into her consciousness. The rest of the characters were in a panic about the sexual experience and it was Sheila's responsibility to keep the facade up, so she appeared snobby and distant.

In graduate school Sheila applied and was accepted to the School of Social Service Administration at the University of Chicago. She felt very inadequate and told her college boyfriend it was a joke. Deep inside Sheila knew the pressure to succeed and perform would be great. She went to prove she was up to the challenge. Working three jobs to distract herself from clinical issues with clients, she was miserable but refused to let her guard down.

Annoyed by her perfectionistic behavior, her life revolved around exercise and vomiting. In her first job at a social service agency, Sheila was aloof and would pretend she knew everything. Her supervisor tried to reach her feelings but hit a brick wall when he got too close.

Recently, Sheila is allowing herself to come out of the act and into her true self. She was always interested in writing and speaking and could never fully concentrate on doing only clinical work. Now all the characters help her with her fatigue and her need to push forward too far. Sheila can rest now and let the other characters rest with her. She's the only "mother" they have and she is a dedicated and responsible adult.

Sheila was continually exhausted because she was over-responsible for others and their growth. She didn't know how to make her own dreams come true. She had seen her clients' lives blossom and grow but had forgotten she had to keep blossoming and growing herself to be a truly effective therapist. She has realized she can go toward her dreams and not lose her business or her sense of self. This is a very new concept to Sheila.

Sheila gives double messages to men as well. When she was a graduate student at the University of Chicago, she was placed at the Jewish Federation and Community

Service Agency in Chicago. Her fellow student intern was a gentle man who wondered how she could throw herself into her work and be so focused and consumed by it. One day this colleague wanted to hug Sheila but she felt angry and wanted to hit him in the face. She didn't want him to know just how much she needed a hug. This is how Sheila operates. She's successful but has a very hard time expressing her hurt and her neediness.

Sheila has always been ambivalent about social work as a career, yet she can hide in it. To distract herself from her pain she took business classes and tried to go to a business oriented job after graduation. She did this because she was afraid her own issues would surface in the social work profession.

Marie: My "Hungry" Part

Out of all of my characters, Marie is the one who holds in much of the rage against my father. She is sixteen years old, very slim, and meticulous about her clothing. She doesn't eat much because she's afraid her body will grow breasts and she'll be voluptuous like her mother. Marie is superficial and will smile even if she's in pain, which is often. She is hungry for love and understanding.

She keeps the abuse cycle going. Every time Sheila succeeds, Marie tries to undermine the progress or to ignore the victory. Marie kicks out any self-esteem Sheila feels. The fighting that goes on between these two characters is evident throughout my junior high and high school experiences. Marie's rage started to come out when she became a teenager. As her body changed, she became more angry, isolated, and protective of space.

Marie felt cold, angry, despairing, lonely, and extremely needy. She's the character that needs revenge and truly hates men. This part of me came out only in codependent relationships, friendships, or on dates.

Marie led a codependent lifestyle. Because she had no idea who she was, Marie was dependent on external validation and approval for her self-esteem. She found little meaning or purpose in her life.

She took a back seat to men, had no assertiveness, and gave away all of her personal power. Marie would want to possess men, to hold them instead of being abandoned, but in her haste to have intimacy, she put sex before friendship and used sex as a weapon she could withhold. She criticized her boyfriends, treated them poorly, and had little compassion for their pain.

Marie confused love with abuse and violence. She confused supervisor and friend. Having no boundaries, she was always allowing herself to be used and manipulated. Marie hated this part of herself and always wished she would die. Because she was a victim, she believed she deserved to be hurt and controlled.

Marie wants revenge at any cost and doesn't care if she is tired, hungry, or unsafe. Although Marie is vain about her body and clothes, she refuses to wear revealing or low-cut clothing. She teases men with her false sense of sexuality but secretly wants to hurt them emotionally. She hides her body and is very controlling. Marie used to think she was crazy. Of course, she's the character who gave specific signals to her fellow student intern to make him want to hug her. Sheila and Marie fight all the time, especially at professional functions.

Marie only feels sexual attraction for alcoholic or abusive men. If Marie is attracted to anyone, she wants sex. Sheila has to protect her from wanting to hurt herself so they have an internal battle going on. Sheila's saying, "Stay away from him," and Marie's saying, "I'm needy for attention," and, "I'd like to go and talk with him." Marie wants to cling to men so she can attack them emotionally later on in the relationship. Wounds can only be healed from the inside out—something Marie doesn't understand yet.

Marie loves to get set up for rejection. She loves to be hurt. She wants to make a large sum of money as revenge against her father because she thinks the money will be the restitution he owes her. Sometimes sadistic in the way she wants to be hurt, her motivation is rage and she is driven to get back at her father. However, the only person she really gets back at is herself. After her sexual escapades she cries and feels like a streetwalker. She feels all the pain again until she gets back in the rage mode and the cycle continues.

In college Marie hooked onto a man who came from Rochester, New York. She treated him badly; she used him. She had to have a steady boyfriend or risk becoming promiscuous. I've had clients who used sex as a way to connect in college. I always remember the pain and the guilt they often feel. For many, they faced venereal disease or some other shaming consequence of their escapades. In Marie's case, she used the relationship with her boyfriend like a shield. Even though she didn't love him or want to marry him, she became addicted to him and was loyal to him.

He wanted to marry Marie but she didn't even know him. He offered her a ring in graduate school but she turned him down. Marie was lost and lonely but Sheila knew the marriage would not be a healthy one. Marie feels sorry she hurt him and wishes she could apologize for her behavior. Marie was so sick with her depression and eating disorder that she had no way to get out of the negative, self-abusive cycle permeating her thoughts and behaviors.

In the more recent past Marie was furious that Sheila was helping teens in therapy while neglecting her. She wouldn't even speak to Sheila and didn't believe Sheila was there for her. So Sheila had to listen to Marie's hostility before she broke down and admitted her own pain.

Sheila is teaching her that competition is another way in which she abuses herself, because Marie is not interested in the process at all. Usually the need to be superior makes her rigid which then makes her feel inferior. She always fails and gets hurt. Sheila has been taking care of her needs and educating her. Marie has been given boundaries and limits.

Teenage Pain

Marie is the character who acted out the eating disorder behavior, and would constantly obsess over male teachers at school. Junior high was a constant battle with depression, obsessing over male teachers, and weight loss. A female teacher told Marie she'd look better if she lost some weight. Marie took her seriously, and lost one hundred pounds in nine months to please her.

She began her binge and purge cycle. Her breath smelled sweet from dehydration. She would get confused, distracted, and dizzy, and then would overeat and feel sick. This continued into her college years and as a young adult. Sometimes she would vomit; other times she'd starve. It all depended on how much she wanted to hurt herself. Marie was so angry that she actually enjoyed vomiting and playing games with the scale.

In her isolation she played tennis against the Junior High school wall for hours on end. Having no limits and no direction, she'd eat five sandwiches when she came home to an empty house after school. She watched television mindlessly and thought about possessing a boy or a teacher at school. Marie was so lonely she used food as a companion. Sometimes, she wished she would die but never did anything else to harm herself.

In school, she was shy about her body, often undressing for gym in the bathroom. She was teased by the popular crowd, who called her "pumpkin ass" or "big mama." She vowed she'd get back at those kids—so when she lost weight between ninth and tenth grade they had nothing more to say. All through high school it was Marie who would debase and defeat herself. She would say to herself, "move your fat butt you cow," or, "you're disgusting, I hope you drop dead." Obviously, Marie had no self-esteem and used negative reinforcement to set herself up for abuse.

Marie Lives with Bulimia and Anorexia

In college and graduate school Marie would vomit and starve periodically. It was so hard trying to hide her inadequate and depressed self and Marie thought that if she starved, she was in control. She developed mind games in her head to prevent herself from eating. Whenever she had a craving for food she'd visualize herself eating it by remembering how it tasted. This gave her a feeling of perfection and superiority.

Many times she would imitate the behavior of her father, who was anorexic for most of his adult life. Marie identified with his bony shoulders and thin physique. Her father was constantly afraid of gaining weight because he couldn't afford to buy new clothes. At mealtimes he mixed all of his food together—like baby food. Marie, however, had a hard time eating mixed food. Her father also had a hand washing ritual and lifted weights in the basement every night after work.

Marie first learned how to vomit from a female athlete in high school. She heard this girl say, "All you have to do is stick your finger down your throat and you lose weight." Marie was already bingeing and starving, so she kept this thought in mind for a later date. She had no idea what damage it could cause.

Marie believed she deserved to be punished for her lack of self-esteem and her imperfections. Vomiting was a way to pay for her mistakes and guilt. She truly felt she was a blight on the world that somehow needed to be expunged. Annihilating herself slowly was the only answer she knew.

In college Marie started vomiting after she had sex with her boyfriend for the first time. All the anger and the abuse issues came right up to the surface. Marie would feel dizzy after sex and very angry. The vomiting continued and the food restrictions got worse. Marie wanted to have sex but abstained for a long time. In her senior year of college she lived with her boyfriend but continued to abstain.

Marie had no way of protecting herself but she did go to counseling. Her counselor told her she did not have an eating disorder while Marie continued to alert the therapist that she did, indeed, have an eating disorder. Marie didn't realize she could change therapists. She continued to progress in the disease process and never spoke about the eating disorder for the rest of the year in therapy.

Vomiting was a very shameful and disgusting habit. Marie vomited every time she had a date in graduate school. Sick and in a daze most of the time, she knew what foods came up the easiest. She even vomited at her field placement agency after lunch. She was addicted to sugar, had mood swings, disoriented thoughts, and was very fatigued.

Marie made it through college and graduate school because Sheila continued to front for her. Sheila was exhausted by Marie's excessive exercise and preoccupation with the scale and with weight. It was very hard to have enough energy to plan for the future. Hence, after graduate school, Marie had no plans. Sheila was lost because she was so busy protecting Marie from exposure that she gave up. This led to the worst 11 months Marie and the rest of the characters ever had.

Marie is the character in this scenario because she had the most power from Junior High until age twenty-five. Sheila didn't know how to get help from the other characters so her only function in relationships was to front for Marie.

Is There Life After Graduate School?

After graduate school Marie went to North Carolina to be with her college boyfriend. They still planned to get married even though Marie had never accepted the engagement ring. She asked where the ring was and he said it "was gone." They did not discuss the situation farther. She didn't love him but was afraid to be alone. He was enjoying graduate school and had recently started therapy to deal with the death of his mother.

A colleague opened her home to Marie so she could stay rent free and look for a job. The agency Marie's colleague worked at had a summer position open but

Marie declined it because she believed the job was beneath her.

Marie moved in with her boyfriend and it was a disaster. This time the relationship became an angry and hostile pastime. Continuing to vomit, Marie became more depressed. She and her boyfriend drove from Chapel Hill to Rochester, New York, for a few days when he had break. His uncle, aunt, and cousin were also there. His uncle had been disabled for many years and didn't want to live. Since his mother had died from lung disease, death seemed to be all around Marie.

They were eating Chinese food one night when his uncle went into the bathroom. Marie could hear him vomiting. When he came back to the table she confronted him in a rage and asked, "Why are you throwing up your food?" The family went wild. That night her boyfriend's father said Marie had to go home.

Marie had to call her father and ask him to send money to ship her boxes home. She'd never felt this humiliated in her life. Her father sent the money but Marie saw it as a failure. Her boyfriend wanted to be a doctor. When asked to help him pay for medical school, Marie declined.

Marie didn't understand that she was deep into her disease. She was projecting the anger and rage she felt for herself onto her boyfriend's uncle. She was so out of touch with herself she didn't realize that what she'd done to his uncle was very wrong.

When Marie came back to New York after graduate school, she was ashamed of herself and her eating disorder. She went to work at a health food store where she was accepted and valued before she had received her Masters degree. Marie applied for jobs in Chicago and considered going back there. She'd stay with the colleague who had offered her a place to stay until she could find a job in Chicago.

She had to start healing and stop her self-abuse. Leaving New York shortly after her arrival there, she got on a plane to Chicago. Although it took her two months to find a job, it took her much longer to heal her heart and function as an adult. She didn't want to grow up but made the choice to go and try to make something out of her life.

Why Look At Our Parts?

Have you ever been in touch with the darker side of yourself? This exploration can be likened to the 4th step of a 12-step process. We need to make "a fearless moral inventory of ourselves." By allowing Marie to speak, I'm helping myself to solve problems and giving the characters in me a chance to work together instead of separately.

When you have no idea what parts of you are in battle, it sometimes feels as if you're in a war with yourself. The only way to go from wounded to wonderful is to explore our dark side and be willing to take off our masks. Most importantly, we need to be honest about our angry, hurt, self-abusive, disappointed, and rejected feelings.

The process we need to go through involves looking at all the parts of ourselves. I have a client who recently attended an anger retreat. A different part of her came out during the sharing exercises. She is very active in a 12-step program and has started a new ACOA group. However, the part she was expressing had never seen the light; she hadn't been in touch with this part. She felt badly because one man in the group suggested she wasn't in a 12-step program because the angry part was so new.

I told her what happened wasn't a bad thing. What was emerging was a split off piece of herself she was not in touch with. She was able to let the part speak, giving her the opportunity of holding on to that piece, exploring that part of her, and integrating that part. Many people wall off angry parts of themselves, especially if they have an eating disorder. When you blockade angry parts of yourself, you self-abuse.

Marie split off her anger and wound up hurting herself. She kept thinking she'd get revenge but she ended up sick and angry at herself instead. The anger backfires. Marie got tired of hurting herself, so she would let others hurt her. Can any of you relate to this pattern? My compulsive overeater's group is puzzled about why they want to punish themselves. They can't understand why they do it.

My experience is that they feel unlovable and don't believe they deserve good things. This can be very unconscious but how many of us sabotage our attempts to gain success, recognition, and love? This is where my self-esteem is the lowest. Marie really feels as if she is invisible. She feels like dirt. She needs to distract herself with revenge because she can't stand herself.

Marie is very much like her father. She needs to alter her depression by restricting food, rigid behavior, and by having obsessive-compulsive thoughts about a man she wants to possess. Other men have told me they don't trust me and I can see why they haven't. Like her father, Marie is aloof and does not allow for any relaxation. She must always pursue a goal. Her father is always moving so he doesn't have to face himself. Marie wants help from Sheila, but doesn't know how to ask for it. Her distractions and self-obsessed wishes for revenge dominate her thoughts. She's a hurt teenager who needs love and understanding. Sheila will be there to help her.

Eugenia: The Beautiful Part

I thought Eugenia was a male character, like my father, so I was very afraid of this character in the beginning. When my therapist asked me to draw my father, all I put on the paper was a black outline of a teddy bear. My father wasn't the monster I thought he was. For all these years, I'd been afraid of a weak and demoralized man. I had almost killed myself over him. He became larger than life somehow.

At first I thought I had my father inside me but when I was able to draw Eugenia, she was beautiful, with blonde hair and golden light around her. She emerged from the cave where she was hiding and behold, she was a girl. Even after all those years of my father calling me "son," I had internalized my identity as female rather than male. I was pleased and surprised when Eugenia came out of the cave.

Eugenia had many holes and deficiencies inside. By letting God fill her emptiness she was able to heal her wounds. She was able to speak and to help me uncover my "sins," and ask for forgiveness and love. Eugenia is the god-self part of me. She is pure love and compassion. She's only a five-year-old and she thinks like a five-year-old—free from prejudices and fear. She's very wise and is the speaker and writer inside me. Eugenia can connect with people and is my biggest asset.

Eugenia is the persona I haven't yet explored fully. She's the part that helps me to hang in there when I feel like giving up. She is translucent and warm. I respect her and yearn to know her better. She has an open heart, an open mind, and loves yoga and relaxation.

Jennifer Pretends to Be a Boy and Wants to Punish Marie

Jennifer is the part of me that is needy and uneducated about everything. She is not a boy but pretends to be one. Jennifer pretends to be Jeff because she believes she'll be closer to her father this way since he hates women. She punishes herself by restricting food when she feels out of control and will terrorize Marie into cutting down on her food intake by telling her that she'll get fat.

Jennifer is mean and punishing just like her father. Her father called her "son" all the time and Jennifer really believes she can be her father's son. She doesn't want to look like a woman and gets upset when Marie starts to grow and gain weight. Jennifer is terrified of living without her rigid structure. Being the loneliest character, she wants no guidance or affection. Jennifer is stubborn and refuses to relinquish the past. She has been hurt by neglect and abuse but refuses to get mad at her father.

Jennifer wants to be a man so much she doesn't care if her father is immoral or abusive. She wants to hold on to any notion of a "father." All the other characters except Marie don't want to be set up for abuse. Jennifer, however, doesn't mind being abused and tries to control and punish the other characters just like her father did. She tries to involve Marie because she knows Marie is insecure. Jennifer loves her father unconditionally and believes she deserves to starve and stay attached to him in any way possible. This makes her special in some way.

Jennifer wants to copy her father's walk, mannerisms, body type, and outside appearance. She wants to look skeletal because that's how he looks. She holds on to any shred of approval from her father. Just to hold on to him, she will even go as far as agreeing with his belief that she is stupid, retarded, or a loser. Although the other parts will not allow Jennifer to contact her father at all, she keeps hoping one day she will bully them enough to be allowed to reconnect.

All the other characters want Jennifer to let go of her hope of ever having a real relationship with her father but she refuses to surrender. This overwhelming and obsessive preoccupation with winning her father's love blocks her from spiritual growth and development. She feels so sad and lost otherwise. She doesn't want God or a higher power to be her father, she only wants her *biological* father. This is very upsetting for the other characters.

Mary: The Inner Child Who Knows What Pain Is

Mary is the character hiding all of my guilt and shame. God seemed to be the only one with the power to help heal her. All the characters had to let her talk and begin to see her as a human being. Mary was living a dead life. She felt numb, frozen, ugly, dirty, and slimy. She looked pathetic and weak and the rest of the characters wanted nothing to do with her. She was not acceptable or valuable. She was self-destructive and full of shame and grief.

Mary was the most hideous thing that ever lived. She looked like an animal—chewing on glass and looking drugged out and unkempt. She smelled and had no hygiene, her hair was tangled, and she looked half-dead. Mary was about four and didn't even know her name.

We didn't want to see her, touch her, or get near her pain. We hid her in a dark cave and fed her insults and criticisms. The characters wanted her dead, but they had to learn to love her and let her speak out about her pain. All the characters had to feel her pain. This was no easy task. Sheila didn't even know she was hiding Mary from everyone until she spoke with a friend after her wedding.

Sheila went to lunch with a professional friend a few months after she was married. This friend asked Sheila what her maiden name was. Sheila said, "I'm glad to get rid of that name, I hate that name." Later, they were talking and the friend told Sheila something about herself. Then the friend said, "But *I* wasn't sexually abused." Sheila was incredulous. She hadn't told her about that. Of course she had, but Sheila didn't realize she wanted to "get rid of" Mary. Sheila did not want to take her father's name. It's not the name Sheila hated, it was Mary she hated. She hated Mary because Mary reminded her of the sexual abuse, something all the characters wanted to repress. All the anger and rage the characters felt about their father was transferred onto Mary. They blamed her for the abuse just as her father had done.

The healing process could only begin when they forgave Mary and had compassion for her pain. Otherwise, they would have continued to hate the part of themselves needing the most help and the part that was innocent and deserving of love and understanding. With a survivor of sexual abuse, this is often the turning point in therapy. When the characters acknowledged Mary's pain, they stopped internalizing the rage. They started feeling anger toward the perpetrator, not toward themselves.

Explaining the Inner Child Process

A friend and I were talking one day. She said her therapist has many dolls in her office and she likes that.

I replied, "I would probably put the doll in a corner and throw darts at it." Then I couldn't believe what I'd just said. I had been doing that for years. Sticking my inner child in the dark corner and doing the same thing to her my father did to me. Why was I hiding her? She didn't even look human to me. She looked like an animal and grunted from time to time. I had no compassion for her. She was worthless, weak, and better off dead. In reality, she was only wounded and once cleaned up, she was not only human, she was the strongest part of me.

This is so hard to tell you because for years I've been hiding my need for help. I would rather slowly kill myself than look at "that subhuman" person who was hurt and violated. My false-self was erected to hide, at any cost, my wounded, bleeding, and severely abused inner child. I also thought if I ever told anyone about my sub-human part, they would have laughed or agreed with me that I was worthless and inhuman. It's possible to clean up and get to know your wounded inner child. The pain is worth it—you won't be sorry.

Although I've read many books describing shame, have spoken to many groups about the subject, and have heard others talk about the feeling of being crazy or abnormal, I've never heard anyone explain its real effects. Sometimes I didn't even know I was feeling shame, for example. Whenever I would say something about myself or let someone know my pain, I always felt waves of shame all over me. It felt like a bad dream and often I looked downward and knew my face was beet red. Shame is hard to share with other people. I've heard it said that if you feel dark, embarrassed, or ugly, it's probably shame you're feeling.

Healing shame and coming out of the cave is also one of the best gifts you can give yourself. As a young girl being sexually abused, there were many times when I felt ugly, unlovable, and broken when in reality, I was abused and neglected. I pictured my inner self as a bloody, needy, and disgusting person who deserved to die—or at least be hidden away so no one would see her. I was so ashamed of what happened to me, I began to internalize the shame as if something was wrong with me, not with what happened to me. I felt like a mistake, a big needy piece of garbage with my hair all tangled and my body mangled and torn. I visualized chewing on glass to get attention. No one would ever come near a person who looked like me, much less accept and love me. My higher power was the only one who loved me in this condition. Because I was so ashamed, I was scared of letting Mary near anyone.

It was God and Jesus who taught me to love my abused, neglected self. It took God's help to make me face her, look at her, and clean her up. I thought she was some kind of monster when truly she was only a hurt, sad little girl who wanted to hold on to someone. I let her hold on to me.

While vacationing in New Hampshire a few years ago, I had a very spiritual encounter. My husband and I went there to climb in the White Mountains and experience the tranquillity and beauty of country inns. I went on my daily morning walk and was enjoying yoga daily. I'm normally not that open to doing these two things but I had the time and there were no outside pressures or demands on me.

I was walking with my headphones on and the song "Open your Heart" by Madonna came on. As I walked on, I felt a very strong presence behind me. I took the headphones off and felt the presence of Jesus himself. I wasn't seeing a vision of him, I was hearing his voice in my mind. I asked if I could help him and he replied that I couldn't. What a codependent thing to ask! However, he replied he could help heal my inner child, Mary. I didn't know what he meant but I started feeling the most intense pain I've ever felt. In my mind I saw my wounded inner self—all bloody, mangled, and torn open in her private parts. I looked at the private parts and cried but it wasn't as bad as I'd imagined it to be.

I know it sounds awful but Jesus said he would help me clean her up. I'd never pictured my inner child as hurt and mutilated before. I went back to the inn and lay in agony on the floor in an unoccupied room. In my mind I saw Jesus helping me wash little Mary. He took the glass out of her mouth and washed her with me. As this healing was going on in my mind I was crying.

He gave me the washcloth and asked me to wash her private parts. Crying uncontrollably by this time, I didn't want to see the blood and the damage that was done to her. Mary was dressed in a white robe and looked almost human. Her eyes gave away her enormous sense of pain and sorrow. It was almost too much for me to bear. Mary cried, and her cry was like that of a wounded animal. It was very frightening. Before, I would never listen to her cry, as it was excruciating and painful to hear.

With Jesus' help, I was able to let her cry and speak. When she spoke, she was calm and not as needy as I thought she might be. She asked if she could talk and I allowed her to tell me what she felt.

After this experience, I worked on healing Mary in individual therapy and in my incest survivor's group. I let her speak her mind, gave her a voice, stopped wanting to do her harm, and stopped feeling utter disgust and pity about her. She wasn't subhuman at all; she was my essence. She was the strong, compassionate one. My other parts had simply dismissed her and prohibited her from getting help, love, and light. The parts inside me condemned my inner child long before anyone else had a chance to.

Mary was accepted by the other characters and today she remains calm, strong, and compassionate. I feel wonderful telling you that I've experienced a healing and a love I never thought possible. Although I have spiritual awakenings often, nothing compares with the day Jesus helped me see and embrace my pain and my humanness.

It was truly a gift from God and I wanted to share it with you. Jesus is the person I saw in this healing experience. He is not the only healer, teacher, or guide who could have emerged. A "Christian" guide or teacher is valid but so are many others. Feel free to put into my story any person or symbol that makes sense to you.

Where I Started and Where I Am Now

Before recovery, Sheila handled everything. Inside, these parts were fighting, condemning, and judging me harshly. Being at war with myself, I didn't feel whole, lovable, or worthwhile. I played this out in all of my relationships. My inner child Mary was the part of me that all of my other characters kept hidden. No part of me would allow Mary to come out of hiding. We were ashamed of her. Jeff (Jennifer) was a mystery to all the characters as well.

Learning how to turn the shame I felt inside out saved me from my own demise. My meditations would tell me I was living a lie—and I had a choice whether to believe it or not. I had to let Marie grieve for the loss of her father and stop looking for men to be her dad. She had to stop using rage to propel her in the world. Marie needed to see her own strength and trust herself. To help her be more compassionate with herself, Marie needed Eugenia.

Sheila had to be helped by the other characters, who had strengths but weren't working together. She had to stop being a workaholic and start being real. She hated being the only adult because there wasn't much support and she had to risk often.

I've Got a Job to Do

I never realized just how much I was hurt, misused, and neglected in my life. I had to accept my inner child, love her, and teach her to laugh, play, and trust others. I let her tell her story without making her feel like a waste or a burden. She told the whole truth to a group of professional speakers in a showcase competition tryout. I lost the competition (only the top 24 went to the showcase, I was number 26) but won back my humanity. It was a small price to pay for freedom. I won so much more for myself when I trusted my gut and allowed myself to tell the truth about what happened in a motivating and inspirational way.

If it hadn't been for the following childhood event, I probably would have killed myself long ago. I made a promise to my grandfather to carry on for him. My mother's father was a teacher in Italy before he came to the United States and was a union steward in the garment district in New York for many years. He was good with people and he was very intelligent.

My grandfather had several strokes in his older years so he came to live with my mother, my brothers, and me. My grandmother came to visit on the weekends. My grandfather loved to read and although he and I didn't speak much, I thought he was interesting.

When I was eleven, my grandfather called me into his room one night, pointed to an end table and said, "Will you take this table downstairs tomorrow?" This seemed like an odd request, but I said, "yes." I was the last person to see him that evening and he died during the night. I heard the cats howling during the night and knew he had died, although I didn't tell anyone I knew this. What came out of this encounter is that I had a job to do. My grandfather had asked me to carry on for him in symbolic terms. I never really took the table downstairs, I merely realized that for some reason my life was meaningful. I truly believe my grandfather is my guardian angel and is protecting me and watching over me while I learn how to empower others in the same way he helped unionize the workers in the garment industry.

Walk Like an Egyptian

During the abuse, I would go to Egypt. I know that sounds crazy but it's true. I'd pretend I was a queen who could control men. The term for disappearing or detaching from what is happening to you during the abuse is dissociation. Many abuse victims separate their mind from their body in an attempt to cope with what is happening to them. This was my defense against feeling the intense and excruciating pain.

In my mind, I would float to Egypt and go to a pyramid. To this day I'm fascinated by Egyptian art, vessels, and pyramids. I would always see a dead queen lying in a tomb with many beautiful gifts, vessels, and light around her. She was beautiful, with dark straight hair and a slim figure. She would talk to me from the tomb, telling me what to do and how to cope with what was happening to me. I thought it was some ancient wisdom, so I would follow it even though I was terrified of being alone with this dead woman in a tomb.

To deal with my fear I would visualize riding an exercise bicycle across the floor from her—pedaling and pedaling to get rid of my anxiety. Let's face it, if you were a child in a room with a dead queen, wouldn't you pedal too? This kept me occupied and took me far away from reality.

There was always plenty of food, water, and air inside the pyramid. The abundance of life sustaining essentials never concerned me. I had no idea why a dead queen would want life sustaining vessels and an abundance of food but I realized later that the queen was not dead—merely sleeping.

I know what you're thinking! No prince was coming to awaken the queen. Only when I admitted my powerlessness years later did this beautiful queen awaken. She was the most loving, kind, and caring person I've ever seen. The bright light around her drew me with such intense emotion I was often overwhelmed. She helped me out of the pyramid and we're now using the gifts and vessels from inside the pyramid to free ourselves from a dead life.

I first traveled to Egypt in my mind for survival. I'd no idea I was tapping into the most powerful resource existing inside each of us. I felt like the dead queen. My mother always told me she died when she got married so I had no role model for womanhood. I thought I too had to die as an adult woman and live a dead life, just like my mother.

The Queen represents the intuitive and powerful part of me. We all have a king or a queen within us. I am no longer a scared child pedaling away my fear and anxiety. By admitting just how powerless and dead I felt, I was freed and no longer lead a dead life. This part in me needed to be awakened. This happened when I took the first step of my ACOA program. My spirituality became the key to unlock my past and stop myself from being afraid of my power as a woman.

I had to reconnect my mind and body, face the pain of my trauma, and see the real impact it had on my life. By dissociating, I saved my life. By admitting my pain, I was able to move beyond my victim role and reclaim the power within me.

After this, I began my search for independence. I used my higher power as my parent and the Queen as my intuition and friend. Both taught me about self-love and how to care for myself. No longer deathly afraid to grow up, I was more honest about where I came from and took responsibility for my life. I realized I didn't lack life-sustaining vessels—there was an abundance of those—and they had been there all the time. This was the beginning of recovery.

Connecting all the parts of my wounded self and putting my two feet on the ground was a slow process. I had to stop waiting for the past to right itself, start building a foundation in the present, and have hope for a prosperous future. I had to use all of my gifts, share them with others, and start identifying with my womanhood. One of my biggest fears was that I would be my mother and not have my own identity. These fears were put to rest as I reclaimed my own life.

Another fear was that if I ever let the light hit my face, others could see what an ugly, wounded person I was. If you are hiding your inner child because you think he or she is ugly, mangled, crazy, or lonely, don't do it anymore. Let your child heal. Let your inner child talk and love that inner child. Let God or your higher power love him or her. Take down the walls a little at a time.

Don't be afraid to live in the light. Underneath shame is a beauty you don't see yet. We've all been hurt but we all deserve to live and heal. Living a spiritual life is the only thing which made me feel secure enough to come out of the pyramid and into the world. I had to leave the pyramid, or I could never have written this book.

3
To Hell and Back

Being victimized is the worst feeling in the entire world. Being made to worship an evil entity is also one of the most inhuman and terror-filled experiences that could ever happen to a person. This is a secret I kept deep inside me because the memories are filled with confusion and helplessness.

I know the difference between good and evil and choose to work for God. I pray for my father but realize he can do something different with his life if he chooses to. In my practice and out in the world, I've found there are more and more people coming out of hiding and sharing this information. I refuse to hide it anymore.

My father now brags about worshipping Satan. I thought if I told anyone, they would blame me. When I hear the word occult, I run away, choosing not to speak with the person. While working on an inpatient unit with adolescents, some of the staff spoke about the power of the occult. I could barely stand to be there.

My brothers, mother, and I don't believe as my father does. My father buys toys for poor children and eats dinner at a church during the holiday season. He also donates money to the church. His confusion is confusing to me. He mixes religion with Satanism and my family and I can never make sense out of his belief system.

In his home, Christian statues and occult symbols were often displayed together. It took me a long time to separate the two in my mind and in my heart. I was afraid of both the statues and the occult symbols. To this day, if I attend a church with many statues, I can't stay there. I also can't have statues in my house at all.

For many years Dad said he could evoke Satan to hurt me and Satan had more power than God. This scared me and I always thought that not only was Dad powerful, he had a powerful force to call on. For years I thought negative things were happening because my father willed it. It took a long time to stop equating negative situations with my father's so-called power.

My father would drink alcohol before any of the rituals began. He would tie me up in his barber's chair downstairs and continue his verbal pattern of torture. I would wonder where he learned all the chanting and intimidation he used to render me powerless. He would chant and make strange noises. By this time he was drunk. He had no friends that I ever saw, but I know he used to go out with some people secretly.

At times he would threaten to burn me with an iron just to prove he could. The occult symbols were spooky and dangerous. He often drew symbols with chalk on the basement floor. My only defense was to pray to God to be saved from this lunatic. It was torture to hear Dad chant the same words repeatedly. This is why I have a very hard time today with repeated patterns or compulsive behavior. Once, I was doing play therapy with a six-year-old child who wanted to play the same game repeatedly throughout the session. This made me so anxious I almost climbed the walls! Even though it was correct for her to find consistency and stability in the routine, I was exhausted.

Since Dad tied me up in the barber's chair with belts, there was no escape route. None. To pass the time, I told God I really didn't mean to renounce him when Dad made me say things like, "I hate you Jesus Christ." Being held in that chair, I only thought of all the good deeds I'd be doing for God when I got out of the chair. Because of this, I can't wear belts easily and can't stand to have anything tight around my neck and upper body. I have to breathe loudly and need space around me to feel safe. These experiences could have ruined my trust in the whole world but I wouldn't let this happen.

Healing and Empowering

In my incest survivor's group, fellow group members would say they felt being a survivor was "a handicap." I had never thought of myself as having a handicap. Maybe that's the reason I can't work with physically handicapped people.

I never realized victimization could affect so much of our lives. Once, I was vacationing in Key West and saw a three-legged dog outside the church we were attending. My husband and I had never seen a three-legged dog before. My heart immediately went out to the dog, who was running just fine on his three legs.

The dog was a golden color and looked like a Golden Retriever. I went to pet the dog, and a Sunday school teacher said, "This is our most spoiled parishioner." Compassion and love were poured on the dog. Even missing a leg, he was still able to live and grow.

As a survivor of sexual abuse, my wounds aren't as visible. I may feel and believe I have no pieces missing but of course I do. I'm just as handicapped as that dog. I lost my ability to experience love and caring, but can still live and grow and move away from the trauma. I want to show you my handicap, not only so you can see the truth, but so I can see the truth as well.

My recovery and subsequent life will always be harder for me because of my sexual abuse. My recovery demands I acknowledge the amount of damage caused by the abuse.

Part of me was jealous of the dog. I, too, share in the pain of suffering and pretended for years to be "fine," while the truth continued to gnaw at my gut. It wasn't until I admitted both my powerlessness and my handicap that I was able to function in an effective way. I had to begin showing myself the same compassion I had for others and let go of my need to self-abuse due to guilt and shame.

I had to come to terms with my suffering. For many years, I felt as if I was hanging by a cross and slowly bleeding to death. I forgot I could be reborn! The past could be thrown away and sent to retreat back into the darkness where it began. I could let go of my shame and my victim status and let in the light. First I had to visualize myself in the light and get out of the chains of guilt and shame binding me to a lifescript I didn't want or deserve.

Why did I feel undeserving of a better life? I had kept a secret to myself for many years. This secret felt so bad I truly thought I'd carry it to my death. Ashamed of my behavior, I've been my own judge and jury. I sentenced myself to life in prison with no possibility of parole. Seriously, I thought I was the worst person in the whole wide world. This is not uncommon, and it dealt with my confusion between sex and violence.

Victimized children often believe the abuse was really love—not an act of betrayal and violence. I learned how to abuse and control others, so that's what I did to my brothers. Also, I was very confused about sexuality, masturbation, and sexual feelings.

I felt extremely stimulated all the time but felt enormously guilty about touching other people. I thought I was gay and didn't realize how normal it is to experiment or to be unsure of your gender identity. I've heard horror stories about parents of my clients who caught cousins or friends exploring each other or playing doctor as children. The children were shamed and made to feel like criminals. If someone had explained this to me, it would have saved me much shame and guilt.

When I was twelve, I found myself attracted to the boys at camp in a desperate way. Not thinking anything was wrong with my impulses, I went out with a boy I hardly knew. He kept negotiating with me, asking me how far I'd let him go. "Just kissing," I said, but couldn't seem to keep this boundary. I allowed him to touch me in other areas, causing me to feel waves of shame and guilt. His older brother became interested in me after this boy told him what I had allowed.

I was very overweight and remember breaking the ladder climbing out of the pool. When I would go to the canteen to get a soda, the person who worked behind the counter would always give me diet soda without my asking for it. I never complained.

Although I wanted to go home, my mother wouldn't let me. Some of the older campers were smoking marijuana every night, but one girl would protect me from the peer pressure by urging me to go to bed before the smoking began. Even though I always went to bed,

I could still smell the marijuana. I was glad the girl protected me.

When I was thirteen, a particular incident happened. I had no idea how to talk about or express my sexual feelings, no boundaries, and no rules about touching, affection, sexuality, and attraction. I was out of control.

Are you holding in a secret that is slowly killing you inside? I felt so much guilt and shame, I thought this was the one thing God would never forgive me for. However, I learned that God could forgive me and now I had to forgive myself.

I admit my behavior was wrong and a big mistake. For so many years, I wanted to hurt myself because I touched my brother. I'm not sure if I touched him, or asked him to touch my genitals. He was only ten and had no idea what was going on. I was home alone with him and knew I couldn't control my impulses or my need to be abused.

For so many years I've remembered my feelings of self-loathing and hate as I asked my brother to touch me. I only did it once because I knew it was wrong. For years, I believed I had hurt him for life. This caused me so much shame that only after being in my survivor's group for seven months was I able to share this secret. I felt they would condemn me. Not only had I been abused, but thought I had continued the cycle and abused my brother. I was just like my father.

Some of you might think this incident isn't very important. Or, you might be thinking how sick I was to engage in this behavior. I guess all I can say is it happened and it was wrong. However, that's all I knew how to do. In relationships, I could be just as abusive to others as my father had been to me. I feel so ashamed that parts of my father's teachings continued to be played out on innocent people such as my brother. After this, I judged myself to be sick and continued to punish myself with food binges followed by starvation. This made me condemn myself.

During my 5th step (which requires us to tell another person the nature of our wrongs), I told a priest about this "sin" and he didn't even focus on the incident. He asked if I was abused and started to connect my "sin" with my pain of being abused. He absolved me of any sin and told me to "go and be a happy girl." It was hard to tell my survivor's group but they were just as compassionate as the priest.

I didn't make amends directly to my brother, since to do so might be unhealthy for him. Instead, I wrote him a letter saying I was sorry if I had hurt him. He replied that I hadn't hurt him and that he loved me. His response made me cry. My own brother told me he loved me after I had treated him like a dog and tried to control his life.

I was watching my brothers when Mom was working but never really showed them any love. I never gave them anything more than I wanted. That position felt powerful, but dangerous. I hated having to be the mother when my own mother was sick and then step down and be the daughter when Mom was well. My mother still tries to hook me into being a parent to my brothers. I took over my parents' roles so often, I can never be a sister to them in the way they need. I'm still finding out what being a sister is.

The chains of sexual abuse are the last to be broken. The secrets, lies, guilt, and self-abuse die hard. I thought I'd never find the key to break the lock. Finally I found that the power of my own love was the key to open the lock.

For so many years, I hid myself because I couldn't look at "the real me," the victim of sexual abuse. I believed if anyone saw this part of me, they would violate and hurt me.

The biggest challenge was to begin to see both my strengths and my weaknesses. I realized that by playing the therapist I was pretending to be self-sufficient. I lived in an image of myself as a rock. The rock inside me was weighing me down. There was so much toxic guilt and shame, I felt like a cesspool. At ACOA meetings, when I felt sorrow or pain, I'd bolt for the door. I wouldn't dare cry in front of anyone. No one was allowed to see the depressed, despairing, and lonely child I really was. I wasn't even allowed to identify with myself. I felt invisible. At aerobics, I had to look at my reflection in the mirror to prove I was there.

Part of me was constantly saying, "Don't you dare admit you made a mistake, were wrong, or apologize." I was so narrow-minded and so closed to healthy resolution of relationship issues that I began to see just how much I needed to protect myself.

By torturing and punishing myself and tightening my own chains, I was engaging in self-hate. My self-hatred had to turn to self-love. This was the only thing that could help the chains to come off and get the rock out of my gut. To begin to breathe, I had to fight each link of those locked chains. I thought I should starve my inner child—just give her bread and water to eat and no pleasures. Was that because Mary enjoyed the abuse? In my heart of hearts, I have to say yes. It was the only kind of touch I knew. So, if I enjoyed it, I must be sick, twisted, and guilt ridden for the rest of my life. Right?

I hated Mary for not spitting in his face, or screaming, or telling another adult who could help me. I believed

I was so evil and sick that I must pay for enjoying the abuse by not having any more pleasures. I no longer allowed myself to explore my body, masturbate, or even think about having affectionate and sexual relationships. If I did have a sexual relationship, I wasn't allowed to feel anything. Hating Mary so much filled my heart with rage, hatred, and sadistic tendencies—just like my father.

When a member of my survivor's group would be absent, I would think it was because of what I'd said the week before. Everyone in the group had a hard time with abuse issues. Finally, I realized I had to spill out all my slimy secrets to heal myself. I got over the fear that my story of abuse would immobilize or contaminate others, but remained afraid of flashbacks or other memories surfacing for me to deal with.

For so many years, I had repressed the memories and buried my feelings in the recesses of my gut. When I got in touch with my anger and expressed it, there was nothing more to fear. I spoke about the rotten and smelly parts of my life and received compassion and understanding. This was the most powerful part of my life. When I think of the harm I caused myself for so many years, I feel sick and sorry.

I abandoned my poor, scared, and hungry self, just as my father did. I left her dirty and a mess and never gave her praise, treats, or comfort. As my own jailer, I was rigid and believed in my own guilt. I'd work myself into a frenzy and then sleep, being so exhausted I couldn't replenish my energy. This has hurt me greatly.

My father's favorite line to me was, "When you fall, I'll pick you up." I would try to fall by pushing myself to the edge of the cliff—but never went over. I'd be damned if I fell down and needed him to pick me up—falling down was defeat. There was a big part of me wanting to fall so Dad could take care of me as he should have before. What an empty fantasy! It led me to nowhere, and I just felt my hunger for love and caring more. Part of me wanted to be strong and prove I was strong, and the other part of me was so weak it was slowly dying. I was living in hell.

Spiritual Guidance

I had my first spiritual experience when I was five years old. This helped me realize my life didn't have to be hell. One night while my mother was at work, my father pushed me down the basement stairs. I don't remember why he did this.

Luckily, I happened to fall on a pile of dirty clothes from the hamper. Otherwise, I would have broken my neck. I prayed to die because I couldn't stand it any more. Immediately, I felt a still, loving presence next to me in the darkness and heard a soft voice inside reassuring me I wouldn't die. This voice continued to envelop me with a loving, calm feeling. I truly felt an angel was with me in the darkness. This was my first experience with being soothed.

Even though I tried to pretend for years that it hadn't happened at all, I was touched by the angel and felt a connection. The angel told me I had something to do in my adult life, so I wouldn't die. The angel left me with a spark of hope which has always flickered inside me. It never went out. I told the angel that if God let me live, I would return the favor and do what he asked of me.

My choice was to unite all of my parts and become whole. All my characters had to learn to work together to grow and prosper. Some parts of me are still mad, scared, wise, needy, and uneducated. I had to learn to identify them, get them to stop fighting with each other, and unite them in love and in peace. I now accept all of these pieces as one. I no longer need to punish Mary and laugh at Marie. Marie has many strengths but is weak in some areas and immature in others. She had to be educated so we all could win. Sometimes the characters fight, but we choose not to adopt my father's sense of reality and evil in our life.

I chose to take off those chains keeping all of my various parts isolated. Removing the chains allowed my characters to start working together. In Key West, I saw an escape artist try to get out of chains in a certain amount of time. Watching him writhe and shake while trying to pry them loose was excruciating and very painful. To make it more challenging, the man was wearing a straitjacket under the chains. He might have dislocated a shoulder while trying to get free. My inner child was cheering him on. He was able to get them off and we all applauded. Some of us gave him a donation; others looked on in terror and fear. I said to my husband, "This is what coming out of a dysfunctional family into recovery feels like."

Survivorship

How many of us have sweated and tried to break our chains link by link to escape our deadness and despair? Was it worth it? Is there life after victimization? A client of mine who recently attended a survivor's meeting was amazed by the number of men who were there as victims. She also noted that no one who spoke talked about a "magical solution" or a cure. We're never cured, but we can rise up and connect with others who have escaped some of the chains and bondage. We can stop protecting the offender and reclaim our lives.

The sun set soon after the escape artist chose, one more time, to free himself from bondage. The sun that set was inside him just the same. We can all have the sun inside us—even as we choose health and recovery one day at a time. My only issue with the escape artist is why did he choose, night after night, to have the chains put on him? After his escape, I saw him sitting by the dock. He looked tired. Maybe it wasn't he who was tired, maybe it was me. I'm exhausted from my struggle to break the chains of depression and misery. I never want to see a chain, much less try to escape from one again. Once is enough!

The next day, I would not go back to the dock to watch the escape artist torture himself again. I feel the same about my life. The past is gone. I can never get it back. I urge all of you to free yourselves from the bondage. Let your inner child out of the darkness and love her or him. I treated my inner child to ice cream the next day. I kept thinking how I had restricted myself for all those years, punishing myself and denying myself treats, pleasures, and love.

Now I'm learning to stop restricting my life and to let go of my old coping mechanisms. They die hard. However, that day I was free, so I celebrated my escape from bondage by letting myself live. Sometimes we all need to rest, eat ice cream, and be grateful and happy for our freedom. Allowing myself a healthy, normal, self-esteem filled life is the best gift I can give to myself. Why punish myself for what others did to me? It just doesn't make sense any more.

4
Spiritual Wake-up Call

Why does it take a tragedy or crisis for us to look at ourselves and our lives? It seems as if when there's a death, I'm more committed to life after grieving. I gain more love and compassion from every person who dies. Slowing my life down enough to see that I'm not immortal, I also realized we don't know how much time we have on earth. All we have is today and our dreams. What were my dreams? If I could do whatever I wanted without thinking about money or other obstacles, what would I do?

Compulsive about everything, I would barely stop to relax before jumping into some project or business scheme that usually left me spinning my wheels. I didn't care because I wasn't in touch with my spiritual hunger then. Hunger always frightened me because I was so empty. Accordingly, I would work to drown out the pain. When faced with my own sense of mortality, I felt the hunger more fully than ever before.

A turning point for me was when the seventeen-year-old brother of one of my former clients died in a car crash. He was the only one of seven teenagers in the car who died. I'd never met him but always had a foreboding feeling whenever his sister spoke of him. I never told anyone about it. Although I can't be sure the conversation actually occurred, he supposedly spoke about his deceased father that night while at a party with his friends. He told others that he didn't fear death. Never could I thank this boy enough for what he did for me. His death transformed my life by causing me to wake up from my fantasy life, face the truth, and start my own grieving process.

Tuesday morning, I was driving home after bowling. I drove past our local funeral home and my inner voice said, "You are going to go to a funeral soon." The last time I'd heard that, it was the truth. I was planning a workshop in April and had asked the boy's sister to be a participant. So, when she called the minute I got home, I didn't connect the two situations. When she said, "My brother died," I couldn't believe it. He was a very popular boy and there would be many grieving teenagers at his wake. I decided to go to be with my former client and her mother.

When I got there, I was numb. Soon afterwards, I felt an enormous amount of pain inside my gut, so I sat down and crunched up on the couch. Beside his casket was a picture of him as a living, breathing human being. The difference was clear. There were Grateful Dead albums in his casket, and this upset me. Was it just the group he loved, or was he telling the world he was glad he was dead? Since I didn't really know him, I wasn't sure. All the teenagers filing in to pay their last respects were crying and it was clear they were unfamiliar with death.

I was furious and wanted to shake him, pull him up, and throw life into him. I wanted to hug him, to put life back in his bloodless body. The anger of being powerless came over me. Seldom had I allowed myself to admit this helplessness. As I sat there feeling cut off and alone, a voice inside me said I was blessed, and there *was* a plan and a purpose for me in life. This message continued to come to me repeatedly. I felt helpless, but calm; I had to begin to trust someone with my life.

Sitting there, I became more aware of my aloneness and compassion. My heart went out to him. The priest said the boy was a tree that had borne fruit. It took me three years to figure out what he meant. The priest then explained that we have no control over our lives—God decides what will happen to us. It's frightening that it took someone's death to help me understand the value and purpose of living. I hadn't been living in the truth. Both in my career and in my personal life, I was playing a role. Although I still could make choices about where I wanted to be in the world, I had many dead pieces inside me.

So, the lesson I learned was that in death there is also life. My client's brother was chosen by God to serve this purpose. It was then I began to realize (just like the teenagers) that we don't know how much time we have. Our time is not limitless. At that point, I looked at the priest's eyes and they were the bluest eyes I've ever seen. I wanted to take the color in his eyes and put it into my dead pieces to awaken them.

This experience began my descent into the inner recesses of my soul and my psyche. I began to notice I was more in touch with both vulnerability and loss. I'd never really grieved for my losses or been totally honest about my feelings.

Spiritual Awakenings

As a young adult, I was in an Anorexia Nervosa and Associated Disorders (ANAD) group. A woman in recovery came to group one day. She spoke about God and said God was the answer. I was furious. Not only did we not invite her out for coffee afterwards, we made fun of her as well. I'm not proud of my behavior, but I was afraid of what the woman had said. She looked so calm and so sure that her solution was working for her. It might work for her but it wouldn't work for me because my eating disorder was unique and different. This denial almost destroyed my recovery process. Wanting to be superior, I didn't want to admit I felt average.

God never stopped trying to reach me. He sent people to my job. He sent someone when I worked at a camp. The woman from camp sent me a bible with highlighted passages. I yelled at her and told her to stop calling me. If someone spoke to me about God, I would nearly go into a rage but didn't know why. I didn't understand why God let all those terrible things happen to me. Having no idea if God would hurt me, curse me, love me, or care if I lived or died, I spent those years in self-induced agony.

Believing I could fix my life with no outside help, I thought I didn't need God. Although I didn't want to admit it, I was powerless. My schoolwork, my *codependent* relationships with men, and my future all evoked this same feeling of helplessness. Admitting I didn't know what to do would be defeat. Struggling and fighting to stay alive, I was certain I'd die if I gave up control. All of my doubts, fears, and insecurities had to be kept inside. Parenting my brothers was much the same—I had no idea what I was doing, but never asked anyone for help. That was losing and completely out of the question.

Can you recall times when you were compulsive about recovery or self-help? Do you feel compelled to read every book about codependency? I'm the type of person who would soak up knowledge and then wait for the reward. When no reward appeared, I felt abandoned by God. Of course it failed; I was trying to play by *my* rules. This made me feel like the biggest failure who ever lived.

Now I realize God didn't forget me. He kept trying in so many different ways to help me but I simply wouldn't listen to him. This makes me sad, because with his love, my life now holds so much beauty and love. There is so much opportunity and joy! Life's a great adventure. When I chose to go back to God, my life started to change and I started to prosper, becoming more human, forgiving, calm, honest, and forthright.

This is the process I went through to develop a sense of self, purpose, and spirituality. I want to make one thing clear—God can't reach you if you don't surrender. You can't keep control and be with God. You can't barter or make deals with God. This sounds harsh, I know, but it's really so gentle and caring. God's will is so comforting, and I trust him fully to help me grow and learn his lessons. He decides what I need and I accept this.

This development of faith and a relationship with God or a higher power is a process. It doesn't happen all at once. It's not a one time decision either.
Whenever I have a problem, I try to turn it over to God. But there I am five minutes later, taking it all back. I forget to use God as a resource and wind up spinning my wheels and getting caught up in my old behavior.

Development of an inner life begins with hope. Sometimes, however, it starts with mistrust, self-doubt, and fear. People who have years of recovery behind them still slip up now and then. This is also a normal part of recovery. When I'm under too much stress, I still obsess over food. Because they die hard, old behavior and habits have to be guarded against.

How did I know and decide that I needed to surrender and get some help? When I couldn't stop crying. I couldn't bear to spend another day in denial pretending my life was happy. I was as depressed as my clients. Many times I wanted to reach out but never thought to look upward. I looked everywhere for help and made some poor choices. I picked people who would hurt me and who had nothing to give. This reinforced my low self-esteem, since I believed it was all my fault. In these shallow friendships, I took all the responsibility and made most of the effort.

I never was happy or had much hope for my life. When I started a recovery program, I realized that by looking upward I could rely on a strength and power which would propel me toward my true purpose in life. God always reassured me that risking myself was the right thing to do, so I turned my focus inward and began to trust my intuition and my inner voice. Before, I had listened to other people, usually men, and let them define and guide me.

With my spiritual development, I began to find my center and believe in my abilities. Before I went on any risky endeavor, I would turn my will and my life over to God, asking only for the power to carry out his wishes. This was like tapping into a gold mine. I began to have faith that I was doing the right thing. My life flowed better and I befriended myself.

I can honestly say that reuniting with God saved my life. Always recreating painful and sad predicaments for myself, I lived from a victim's standpoint. Letting go of old wounds and angry resentments was difficult for me. The first time I surrendered to the higher power, it was a tremendous effort. Part of me didn't want to admit I needed help. That part cursed God. I could hear the struggle going on as the healthy part of me wrestled the other part to the ground and made it "cry uncle" and surrender. Feeling as if a demon had been released from me, I cried and moaned.

Sometimes I wonder if the reluctant part inside me was my father's belief that the power of the devil is greater than the power of God (at least that's what he told me). Not only had my father threatened me, he'd also had an unseen force threatening me. With this larger-than-life force, I felt totally devastated. The rituals didn't seem all that strange, it was more the black cloud I felt was always hovering over me. Since Dad had said that Satan was stronger than God, I began to believe it. Now I choose not to believe it and don't have to live with the black cloud over my head anymore. There is no unseen force trying to murder me. God loves me and I am protected by his love.

When I chose to surrender my will to God, I didn't know if God would hurt me or help me. It was like falling off a cliff into nothingness. But I landed on solid ground and began to heal my life. Accepting that I needed help from a power greater than myself was the turning point. I realized that where I thought there was nothing, I had created something. Facing the nothingness and emptiness enabled me to head in the right direction. I created this book and I created a life for myself. I'm free from my past persona. I am myself and can fill myself with goodness.

The abusive part inside me that was my father died. I wasn't going to pretend to like being self-abusive anymore. Why couldn't I have a happy life? No one in my family ever told me I could, but I knew it was out there. I had to start looking upwards instead of everywhere else. Based on prosperity and abundance concepts, I can create the kind of life I deserve. I now take full responsibility for creating positive, worthwhile, and loving relationships with the world, the church, my clients and friends, and myself. I feel as if I'm a different person. It seems odd to me when I think back to the way I was living before. It's unbelievable that I chose to live a painful, depressed, and empty life.

So you see—there is a way out of your pain and self-abuse. Surrender your life to the higher power. Turn your life inward and upwards. Start believing in this power which is greater than you. Make a connection to God and tell him if you're angry. Don't run away from the truth. It hurts but will set you free. Learn more about spiritual development and honor your inner voice. Claim your legacy and accept God inside you. Share dominion over the earth with God. Love others, create positives for yourself, and be yourself.

Spiritual Journal

Meditation helped to show me I was living a lie. Many times my inner voice urged me to get rid of dead roots and replant myself in another career. When I examined my current lifestyle, I saw that my roots were dead but my spirit was alive. This was illustrated in some of the intense visualizations I experienced. In them,

I was in lush, green places surrounded by people applauding. A book was in my hand and I was smiling.

My spirituality evolved out of the New Age thinking process until I was able to grow and use more of my 12-step program. Also, I began to start believing my inner wisdom would continue to emerge.

Other messages such as "energy flows from those who know his power," and "trust in your own strength" are consistent with the divine being within me. After hearing and writing these phrases, I felt completely taken care of. When I needed guidance, I'd go over these messages. By asking for help, something I'd never have done in the past, I could tap into that energy. This gave me a renewed sense of serenity and peace, and awakened in me new feelings of joy and freedom. So I could hear the power in me, I taped my voice while going through this process. I'd never listened to myself before, so this helped me tremendously.

The meditations continued and the messages always urged me to have faith in my abilities and to continue the journey. My higher self told me I have the key to salvation and would use it to help spread energy to others. When I asked about my need to hold on to codependent relationships, the messages stated I would need to give them up. My higher self also explained that my creative spirit would overtake my rigid structure. This helped me end relationships in which I had lost myself. I realized that when I let go of other people, I could have my own power and have trust in my inner voice—two of the greatest gifts I could ever receive.

However, my fear of being infused with evil or negative spirits haunted me. I was continually afraid these messages were coming from a dead spirit or that someone was inhabiting my body and telling me some old garbage. These words, however, reassured me, "We are not some dead spirits waiting to use your body, we are highly evolved pieces of you that grow with your permission and guidance." In other words, I had a choice whether to use the information or not.

My inner self seemed very wise and interesting, but it was hard to understand how I could have an inner self so full of wisdom. I asked where these highly evolved pieces came from. The answer was, "In your case, life experiences and much time spent alone on fantasy related projects for coping with present destruction. We take away the fantasy and build on your structure."

My higher self (the Queen) told me that I had worth, value, and a life purpose. I felt protected and loved. This was better than any other substitute parenting I'd ever had. It enabled me to plunge deeper into the recesses of my inner self and locate more strength and power. The River Within is strong, secure, and mighty. I feel as if some ancient wisdom is on my side as well. This oasis inside me is ever flowing and true to my own well being. New energy is always aligning with me to create more meaning and purpose in my life. I began to ebb and flow like a river, and to tap into beauty, serenity and, inner wisdom.

When I wouldn't consult The River Within, I lost vital information that could help me. I kept believing this was too good to be true and sometimes doubted that I deserved all of this beauty and wisdom. Sometimes I forgot to consult The River Within—choosing instead to listen to my chatterbox and negative thoughts. During my spiritual struggle to accept God as a living entity inside me, I also examined my frailties. My fear of failure and my history of sexual abuse stopped me at various points in my spiritual development.

One such defect was I trusted others more than I trusted myself. Another was I tended to pick friends who were critical and not supportive. I realized I'd replaced food with countless codependent relationships, and still believed I would never have good things or an abundance of anything.

Believing in my own uniqueness was hard for me. I always thought my life would be a constant struggle for survival, and who would I be without it? The thought scared me. I had to give up my treadmill existence. Would I gain fifty pounds? Would I become lazy? No, I'd become happy and relaxed. This was the goal, anyway, but I'd no idea how I was going to get there.

My inner voice would tell me how. On many occasions, I heard, "Seek the love inside the home of your voice. Grow with the knowledge of the divine. Love thyself and all your imperfections. Love others. Seek no retribution." During these meditations, I felt the light inside me burning brightly—not just flickering.

Choosing a Spiritual Life

What is a spiritual experience? It begins when you learn a life lesson and your mind expands. It's a spiritual experience when anyone gives you a compliment or gift. When you feel a connection and a sense of belonging, that's also a spiritual experience.

Have you ever been out camping with the scouts? Remember any camp experience and you'll find spirituality. Nature provides the quiet and beauty for renewal and a heightened sense of purpose. If you think back on your life, you'll surely begin to see you've been on a spiritual journey all along.

Remember any turning points in your life. You had no way of knowing how a certain decision would turn out beforehand. Yet you chose one path over the other for some unknown reason or gut feeling. These turning points are spiritual experiences because you couldn't have known the outcome. Think of times when obstacles seemed to fall out of your way. These times felt natural and easy compared to other events. Those times were spiritual in nature or higher powered in some way.

I've an exercise I give participants in all my workshops. Based on turning points in their lives, I ask them to plot their spiritual journey. Try this and see how your spiritual path has been evolving. Another way to plot a spiritual journey is to note when you are fully aware, alive, or passionate about a certain issue or activity you are involved with.

People can also bring you spiritual experiences. For example, I was very unsure of my speaking ability at first. But I received such a great response I decided to go into professional speaking. One day, I was feeling so down and unsure that I asked God for a sign in this regard. Out of the blue, my friend Jan left a message on my answering machine that night about what an excellent speaker I was! This encouragement gave me the motivation to go on despite my doubts and fears.

That was truly a spiritual experience because it made me aware of a higher plan for me. Think of times when others have brought you some kind of news that validated, encouraged, or supported you to move in a certain direction. Have you been helped by strangers who have given you information which led you to the next step of your plan or goal? I'm not saying you should wait on your doorstep for people to come to you; you must do the footwork. Taking active steps to move in a certain direction is a spiritual experience.

People are afraid of the spiritual dimension because it's unknown and mysterious. No one knows exactly how a 12-step program or a spiritual journey progresses. Even the most intuitive can't understand what's happening inside. Shifts in values and thoughts happen gradually over time. It's amazing how the spiritual process changes you. You will need to open up to this unknown dimension and value it once you see it work for you. You'll need to begin to focus on your own life, trust your inner voice, and learn how to claim the power deep within you.

One can tap into spiritual experiences by getting quiet and taking time to relax and contemplate. Thomas Keating in his book, *The Heart of the World*, believes people experience God but don't talk about it because others might think they're crazy. He goes on to explain that it's normal to be contemplative and we need to cultivate this skill. One can learn to meditate, do yoga, take relaxation classes, get a massage, or simply enjoy a trip into nature to contemplate and speak with God.

My sister-in-law believes in the spiritual process. We communicate by asking each other, "What has God been telling you lately?" Don't be afraid to admit you talk with God, a serene and healthy process. Don't let society's discomfort stop you from talking with God directly. A helpful technique is to write down all the gifts, compliments, and positive things you receive daily. Make sure you include the date. By the end of the week you'll be amazed at how much goodness the universe has given you. If you focus on what you *do* receive, not what you don't receive, life is so much more positive and supportive.

Every experience which makes you feel good, connected, affirmed, happy, or peaceful is a miracle in itself.

I'd love to hear your spiritual stories. These are very important to share with each other. We need to share with one another without thinking we're crazy or that we need to be alone with our pain or our joy. Let's share the love we have inside with others. This is the true essence of spirituality.

A relationship to the higher power is open to everyone but few people make the choice to follow the spiritual life. Each of us is special. It's a matter of trust, faith, and self-worth that leads us deeper into our spiritual journey.

Think about times in your life when you didn't know how, but everything worked out fine. When have you followed your intuition and been pleasantly surprised? Even if you weren't taught anything about religion or spirituality, you have it inside you. All you need to do to grow is acknowledge your innate spiritual self.

A good friend of mine gave me a card with these words, "Relax, God's in charge." How many of you would be terrified by that? As a spiritual teacher, I have struggled with this on a daily basis. Putting your life in the hands of a higher power is scary and a big leap of faith. When I felt out of control, I had to remind myself that I don't need to have control. Clients who get frustrated with this try to fight and keep control. This is a normal and ongoing part of the process.

I decided to face the truth about myself and admit I was powerless. I wanted to stop living a lie because I was not only afraid to die, but afraid to live. For years I'd felt dead. Non-living is what I call it. I worked, slept, and existed—that's all. John Bradshaw, in speaking to the crisis of the family, states that we don't know who we are. I simply didn't want to go to my grave a shell—living out someone else's identity.

All of my life I've been on both personal and professional journeys. The journeys are not totally separate, so it's hard to distinguish between them. Both deal with survivor and codependency issues. While reading this, remember that my personal and professional journeys have intersected. This is why I'm writing *The River Within* as I am. The point I'd like to make is the same point John Bradshaw made in answer to a letter I'd written to him. He told me the best thing I could do to help my clients was to do my own shame work.

This means I needed to look at myself as a person. Hence, I've become a better therapist. I would add that parents can become better parents by looking inside themselves and dealing with their own wounds, needs, and fears.

On the advice of my therapist I chose to go to a 12-step meeting. I had no friends and had heard a 12-step group would hook me up with others and help me feel less isolated and different. There, I found relief, power, and a sense of friendship I'd never felt before. The program helped me move into speaking as a career and put me in touch with my inner child. The meeting I chose to attend was for Adult Children of Alcoholics. People with mentally ill and dysfunctional families are welcome at these meetings.

More Spiritual Experiences

On our trip to the Grand Canyon, I experienced exhilaration and fear. I was walking and felt the need to be secluded. Feeling almost giddy, I started to laugh. When my husband started to point out something of interest I told him to leave me alone. I continued laughing and walked to a solitary place and sat down. "You will be a household word by the age of forty," my inner voice said. At the time, I was not yet thirty. Of course, I started to feel powerful and happy that I was going to amount to something great! I still have no idea what the message meant, but it felt good to hear God and my inner guide tell me this. The Queen always disseminates ancient wisdom to me.

While traveling in Arizona, I've gotten in touch with my spiritual self. What it was about Arizona that attracted me there I have no idea, but I've received the strongest spiritual messages and peaceful times there. Although I had never heard of Sedona, Arizona, my husband said it was a beautiful place. I was slightly nauseous and wasn't looking forward to stopping to see the town but I'm glad we did.

As we entered the town, I felt powerful energy as well as spiritual messages coming from the place. In a gift shop I saw an arrowhead necklace and became so drawn to it that I bought it. Just a few hours before, we had been in Flagstaff, where I'd felt very negative about the place we were staying and had been constantly tired and had nightmares.

When the car pulled into Sedona, however, my physical symptoms went away and I was filled with energy and vigor. It was like being caught in a magnet. We went into another gift shop. Something told me to "spread my money around," so I bought a candle and other artifacts. An energy seemed to vibrate inside me.

Walking into a store to buy some soda, I knew I didn't have enough money to buy two. I kept counting and recounting my money. All of a sudden, there was enough for the two sodas. That store made me feel like I was in a time warp.

At another store I bought some red and brown beads. Usually it's very hard for me to spend money, but I was buying things left and right—enjoying the freedom and energy this place brought me. It was almost as if my inner self was taking over and leading me in a certain direction. I felt safe, protected, and totally trusting in this environment.

I was told the beads ward off evil spirits. For protection, I put them around my neck immediately. I knew I'd learn something about myself in this place, which seemed magical and mysterious at the same time. Something special and powerful was happening below the surface here. The red rock was beautiful—and nestled in the red rock was the town. I marveled at the different shapes of the red rock, which seemed so inviting.

We stayed an hour or two but it seemed like only a few minutes. Leaving was like saying goodbye to an old friend. Driving away, I saw people climbing the red rock. Feeling protected, I knew I wasn't meant to climb. I started to talk to my husband about my spiritual experience.

I said that souls were very close and began to open up an area deep inside me. This area appeared to be wiser than I. I told him about the message I received at the Grand Canyon and how I've always felt protected by some positive force or inner guide. I couldn't stop talking about this hidden part of me. It was a huge portion of me, but I'd never tapped into it or explored it in any depth. Also, I spoke about times in my life when strange things happened. For example, as a child I got my fingers caught in a car door. Yet, when I looked at my hand, none of my fingers were crushed.

When we arrived back in Phoenix, we went into a bookstore. There was a book about Sedona and how it is a spiritual center. There's an energy vortex there I had no idea existed before stumbling onto this place. The vortex is like a giant crystal underneath the earth which draws energy and is powerful. There are only a few such vortexes in the world, Sedona, Arizona, included. There are many spiritual stories about Sedona, including one about the ancient city of Lemuria. If you're interested in learning more about the vortex and Sedona, many books are available on these subjects.

California Dreaming and Meditation

Until I meditated at the Oaks spa in Ojai, California, I didn't even know I had an inner voice. It was my first time in yoga class. I got quiet enough to hear, "You will make a fortunate turn." At first I dismissed the inner voice as "craziness," but now I know the best friend I was always looking outward for was right inside me all along.

The fortunate turn I'm in the process of making is my love and devotion to the spiritual lifestyle. Out of touch with my needs and my inner resources, I had been living a codependent lifestyle. The experience at Ojai was the first time I realized I had an inner voice who could guide me in a positive way.

5
The Recovery Road

Once upon a time there was a girl named Shame. Shame hid in the darkness and slept during the day. She looked like an ugly, nasty monster in the light. Light was her greatest enemy. Shame had a heavy and closed heart. She held in many resentments and felt enormous fear.

Shame grew up in a family where everyone lied and pretended they loved one another. They would fight and yell and cut each other up with criticism and teasing. Shame was lost and neglected and felt unlovable. She never opened up to people and spent her life in a self-made prison.

Self-hate and Fear, Shame's brothers, also hid in the darkness. They all went through school pretending to like themselves. All three spent much energy trying to be invisible, never wanting any attention focused on them for fear that others would see them as the monsters they really were. They had few friends—no light would ever shine on them.

Just in case she made a mistake, Shame never took risks. Mistakes were forbidden by her parents—so were anger and sadness. Shame's only fun was going at night to the other side of town to walk around. On the other side of town no one bothered her. One night, she was walking in the other place and came upon a prophet. His name was Love. Love was a beautiful person who told her a secret. He told her if she found a person named Light, she would be led to the recovery road. If Shame went down this road with Light, she would find peace, happiness, and self-acceptance. Shame asked, "Why are you telling me about this road?"

Love responded by saying gently, "Because you deserve to be in my village of love." The recovery road can take you to your true self and your potential as a human being. This road is open to anyone who chooses to embark on the journey of love. Shame did not believe this man. When she asked for proof, Love said all she had to do was ask for Light to come and guide her. She had to admit she couldn't find the road alone. Along the road, Light would help Shame open up her heart and clear out all the fear and resentments that were eating her up. Otherwise, Shame was free to choose her present lifestyle for good. It was her choice. Love said if she got on the road, she would know an inner happiness she had never thought possible.

Shame grappled with the idea and used all kinds of logic and rationalizations to get out of it. Light was her worst enemy! She'd have to throw out all of her old beliefs and replace them with new ones. The thought of doing this was very strange, but she toyed with the idea and kept hearing the faint beating of a heart. As she was speaking to Love, it got increasingly hypnotic. Frightened, she said, "I don't believe you, Love!" and ran home. Trusting others was not one of her strengths.

That night, Shame had a strange dream. She dreamed she was in a beautiful castle with her best friend Light.

The streets were lined with people who looked like Love. In the light she was no longer ugly and didn't look like a monster. Just the opposite, she looked like Love. Feeling accepted and loved by all the villagers, she followed the beating of the heart into the castle. She went to the bell tower and there, standing in front of her, was a person who looked exactly like her. This person was a Queen. She was dressed in the finest of silk, had long straight black hair, and the most beautiful, radiant smile.

She said, "I'm the part of you that shines underneath your darkness." She went on to say, "Find the recovery road and walk with Light. Do not be afraid of Love or the road. Light is your friend, not your enemy. Travel this road to the top of the castle and claim your true self. Trust me just this once." Shame marveled at her beauty, her firmness, and her wisdom. She was amazed by the Queen's artistry and compassion. When she reached out to touch her, the woman disappeared. Shame awoke in a panic.

She got up in the day and ran to the other side of town as fast as she could. At first she asked for Love to come to her and then she screamed, "Love, come to me! Love, come to me!" Love appeared and was calm and concerned. Then she asked for Light to come by saying, "Bring me Light, bring me Light, bring me Light! I can't find the road by myself! I need your help." Shame had never asked for help with anything.

Light appeared and Shame was immediately transformed into a ray of light. She felt protected and safe but the light was too bright. Shame hid her eyes and said, "It's too bright, it's too bright." However, she was able to squint enough to see Light smiling at her and offering her a hand. She took Light's hand and the two walked to the recovery road. To get onto the road, a password was needed. Light told her to say it. Shame said, "I don't know what it is." Light assured her she did know it. Shame thought for awhile and then blurted out, "I'm human. I make mistakes." This was the password and they walked onto the road.

The recovery road seemed like any other road. But it had something that not all other roads do. It was winding and chock-full of obstacles, traps, and pain. They passed some people who were crying; others asked for hugs. They told the truth and showed their true feelings to one another. This road was full of compassion and understanding, something Shame couldn't even give to herself. Shame and Light walked until they came to the outskirts of a city called Patience. There were many people lined up waiting to get inside. Some were angry because they had to wait. Others accepted it and camped out in the wilderness.

Patience guards opened the door for Shame and Light immediately. They found Love seated in the town square talking about philosophy and ethics. He said, "Welcome to the village of Patience. Few choose to come here by faith alone.

Others can't wait to get in and leave bitter and angry. No matter how long the wait, it's necessary. People don't seem to understand that they arrive when it's their time—no exceptions. It is your time. Go serve your fellow man and tell everyone about your faith. The Queen is waiting for you with further instructions." Light didn't need to go so Shame went alone.

The Queen was sitting on her throne. When she saw Shame, she reached out to hug her. Just like Love, she was very wise. Her name was Higher Self. Higher Self told Shame to spread the love and light to others, and to be a guide for others seeking the recovery road. Higher

Self was pleased with her and told Shame she was within her always. Higher Self explained she was Shame's guide and would lead her toward healthy, happy paths. Shame felt full and calm. This support was unlike any she had ever known. She thanked Higher Self and went to relax in the nearest pool. Now, her mission was to teach others how to find and use the recovery road.

As she was walking toward the pool Higher Self said, "Explain to others how Love helps to heal shame, fear, and self-hate." Shame promised to make a commitment for the rest of her life to serve Love and to take Higher Self with her on her travels.

Spiritual Concepts and Connections on the Recovery Road

The story speaks to how we can discover, accept, and become our true selves. Our true self lies within us and can be called our "God-self." This God-self is a mighty higher power and has only good intentions for our growth and development. Shame is a universal feeling but so is the God-self. All human beings have the potential to find the right road and to find out who they really are. God calls us to this task. God is always reaching out for us to return to his love and reconnect with him. He's given me numerous chances to reunite with him. I'm the one who wouldn't relinquish control and greet him with an open heart.

Shame doesn't seem to have much resistance to the idea. In a recovery program, the resistance is much worse and more pervasive. Those who want to prove to themselves they're not addicted to a substance, activity, or person reject this reality. If we charted it, Shame would take a much longer time trusting Love or a higher power in recovery. The concepts of "a leap of faith" and "letting go" are important here. The higher power can't be seen by the naked eye—so faith is the only proof there is. Letting go of control is hard, as Shame was made aware through a dream.

The story also speaks to the higher consciousness of our world. The concepts I've used are universal in nature. What we are all trying to do is transcend our ego boundaries and become one with our universe. I call the core of our being the God-self, or the Higher Self. This part is not only the most powerful part, it is the most loving and compassionate part.

Bradshaw speaks about our "unity consciousness," which means that nothing outside ourselves will make us happy. Our home is deep within us and only an inner life will lead us to happiness. An addictive life does not bring us happiness. There are many false Gods leading us by greed, manipulation, or fantasy deeper into our search for external validation. When we begin to understand these false gods don't lead us to paradise, we start to believe we've been duped. The false gods look good—but anything that looks too good and easy is probably an illusion.

Therefore, Shame became someone different when she asked for Light to come to her. Shame was transformed into someone new. This is our true self and we need to understand that we can be transformed into a new self. By having an inner life, we create an existence filled with joy and serenity. Dreams are also important to discuss, as the subconscious often leads us to the next level of thought needed to pursue the goal of knowing ourselves better.

Understanding the Recovery Road

When I had no sense of spirituality, I mistrusted my motives. I carried other people's burdens and was angry, depressed, and hated myself. I had so many fears and so little support. I had an incredible drive, but this was often rage turned inward. There was no purpose or meaning connected to my life. I couldn't see past the black cloud that rained on me and kept me depressed and lonely.

I was too busy playing a role I didn't write for myself. My parents wrote the script, and it was a miserable one. I never questioned this lifescript because I enjoyed hiding in the darkness. The darkness became my friend and my protection against outside forces. I was very strict with myself. My only goal was to survive—not feel alive and happy.

When darkness became my home, sunlight became an enemy to be avoided. If I allowed others to see the real me in the light, I thought they would hurt me. Being invisible meant I didn't have to explore myself. In my darkness and despair, I saw my life as a pathetic attempt to imitate other people I admired—wanting their identity, not my own. I dissociated from my real self and gave myself no compassion, no self-care, and no love.

My intuition told me to proceed with recovery, but my shameful self cried out from the darkness, "Don't you dare admit any mistakes." My dark side was warning me to not break the rules and try to change the lifescript. As I became more understanding of my lack of power, I realized my inner voice of despair was preventing me from healing. Finally, I realized I deserved to heal. Facing the truth became my exit from of the cave of darkness I was living in.

The story of the recovery road is the story of the 12-step program. I've focused here on parts of the program that are very difficult. I created the story about Shame to illustrate The River Within all of us. The characters are all parts of recovering people, myself included. These parts are easy to identify in the story. Are you aware of how these parts operate in your life?

Perhaps you can identify those feelings you are "stuck" with. They get in your way of believing in a higher power, or a place inside yourself of pure love and compassion. The main point of the story is to exemplify the resistance to admitting that one is powerless and in need of help from an outside force. This outside force is something we're afraid of because we need to trust it and give up control. We don't know what we'll encounter if we ask for help from a power greater than ourselves. How many of us have been our own Gods, or have given that distinction to another person?

Look for parts of the story you identified with as you read it. This is one way to embrace a recovery process. The miracles come only when we allow God, our higher self or our higher power, to help us.

The concepts of darkness and light are themes in many fairy tales and literature. There are dark parts in each of us we don't wish to see. If we believe in the wholeness theory, all of our parts can operate together. There's no need to hide or split off the dark side of our personality. They are just parts needing our help and attention.

When we are in recovery, we need to use more of our heart energy. Heart energy is the compassionate part of ourselves that counteracts darkness and despair. Heart energy is healing—while darkness is not. Shame's story speaks to the heart energy in all of us, and the ability to make a transformation from darkness to light. When Shame was transformed into light, she became her true self. Everyone needs to realize we can be transformed into our true selves by releasing shame and developing our compassion and self-love.

The part of us that is love, God, hope, or pure energy is with us always. In the village of Patience there is no hunger, famine, pain, or suffering. Everyone is accepted. There is no toxic shame and guilt. This is the most fertile part of The River Within—full of lush plants and vegetation. This storehouse of love, wealth, and strength is our true essence. The spirit prevails and the love being shared is spectacular. We can all get to this part of ourselves. In bible literature, this is similar to the land of milk and honey Moses was looking for after leading the slaves out of Egypt.

Light can melt the rock or ease the burden we may feel deep in our hearts. An open heart is needed to get to the road and the village. I have an audio tape from the Jungian Storyteller Series entitled *Warming the Stone Child.* Clarrissa Pinkola Estes tells stories about abandonment and children who were not nurtured or mothered. She hypothesizes that some of the best healers in the country had little or no nurturing or mothering as children. She speaks about the different parts in each of us—some light and some dark. We are innately intuitive, she says, and we can sense danger. There is something deep in our soul that allows us to survive despite the obstacles.

Abandoned or severely abused children must believe in some lighted place inside them that embodies a sense of hope about their future. This lighted place is the village, Patience, which waits for us with open arms. There is an ancient wisdom inside us that guides us from the darkness. We fear this part of us is evil but it's merely a strong inclination to get us to the light.

During my life, I've both succeeded and failed. At first, I didn't consciously know what was enabling me to survive, but I later realized it was my will to live in spite of the pain and devastation. Everyone has had obstacles to overcome. Our essence is to survive, and thrive after we find our home—deep inside The River Within. The recovery road is the road of happiness we're all looking for. The road can't be seen just by opening your eyes, you must open your heart as well. You don't have to travel to distant lands to find love, light, peace, and happiness; the recovery road is inside you.

Many adult children from dysfunctional or alcoholic homes are afraid of the light and love. Some of my clients stop me from giving them any positive comments because they can't integrate goodness inside themselves. They don't want to "take in" the goodness and the warmth of the light.

For so many years, I had lost touch with my essence and refused to accept the good inside me. One night early in my recovery program, I received a message. It was 11:00 P.M. and I had an overwhelming urge to get up and turn on the television.

I knew God wanted me to hear something. The program was about incest. A priest was talking to a survivor about the experience. The priest explained that we should never let human experience destroy us. He continued by saying there is a living God inside us who works mysteriously to heal. Something inside me connected like iron to a magnet. I realized I had to stop living the lie and face the truth. This was no easy task. As a professional, I had to let down some of my facade and let others see the real me.

What's underneath the darkness inside us? A friend from ACOA recently gave a talk on control. He was terrified because he felt confused and didn't want to admit it. A lady in my sharing group said she was more controlling when she didn't trust herself. Since darkness can be equated to shame, and the light with God or a higher self, we have a choice. Underneath the shame is a diamond, and an inner beauty we never thought possible. If we trust our higher power and turn the shame inside out, we can find a part of us that is wise, all-loving, positive, and can guide us toward our greatest good. We need to allow our shame to surface, trust God, and let go of control.

Let me be honest. Choosing a spiritual life opens up your pain, breaks down your isolation, and joins you to a power that knows what's best for you. This is a scary thought and a painful journey. However, if you ask any recovering person about the program, he or she will tell you it saved his or her life.

A client of mine recently completed almost three years of therapy. She was a compulsive overeater and incest survivor. She wrote down where she was before therapy and a 12-step program and where she is today. She stated the spiritual part of her recovery was the most important element in her life. Before therapy and the 12-step program she would seclude herself at home with food and fantasize about the times she could eat alone. When she was hurting, she pretended all was well. Does this sound familiar to you?

Don't continue to mask your true feelings with a smiling face, you don't have to keep up the performance. My client told me honesty was the freedom she needed, along with my guidance and safe places to be herself. Her spirituality will continue to grow and she'll continue to prosper. Because she could acknowledge God in herself, she was able to see God in me. The spirit in one always perceives the spirit in others.

It's wonderful to hear her speak about herself in the present as a living, loving, and supportive person. In my private practice, I've witnessed tremendous growth and maturity in recovering clients. Not only do they find relief from their obsessions and addictions, they begin to value life. You can be part of a living, thriving community, or you can live a dead and despairing life. I chose to walk on the recovery road and found my soul. Human experience will never destroy me.

Spiritual concepts can be explained by various symbols in the story. The beating heart signifies how God tries to reach out to us and let us know he's close by if we choose to call on him. God always reaches out to us through other people, stories we read, or even by directing us to view certain movies or television shows.

Now, I'd like to discuss those who are impatient to get to the city. Many of us want recovery now and we want it our way. As the story says, you can only enter the city of Patience when God decides to let you in. Also, you can meet other travelers on the road and learn from them. Each person on the road gets protection and love from God and learns about humility, surrender, and joy. The recovery process is for life. We try to help others on the road enter the city of Patience, which is our true self. Our true self gives us strength, identity, and energy and holds our potential as human beings.

The concept of co-creation applies here. I think of co-creation as a silver thread connecting our higher self and God. One can have profound insight and wisdom from this level of thinking and being. All the different parts of ourselves are united and synergy takes over where fragmentation and splintering once were. The city of Patience is a heaven on earth, so to speak.

To be successful, we need to get in touch with and learn to trust our higher self. Like an inner guide, this self often knows what is best for us. It always creates, offers love, and speaks the truth. It is up to each person to choose this resource. The queen in the story represents our higher self or intuition. She asked Shame to trust her just this once. To embark on a recovery program, we must trust our higher self because we can't control outcomes. Somehow our higher self or queen is offering us insight into the future, so we need to have faith in our own instincts and hunches.

A spiritual turning point happens when we move in a direction out of choice without knowing in advance what will happen. This is trust. Our higher self has been guiding us for a very long time. What made you choose to move in one direction instead of another?

Love is the symbol for the higher power or God. Light is God's protection and grace. The concept of shame is universal because our shame represents darkness and keeps us from loving ourselves and the world. On the road, we learn how to deal with this shame, expose it, and turn it into love. The recovery road always helps us turn negative events or turning points into positive, healthy, and self-esteem building opportunities.

Dream work can uncover the unconscious ways in which we operate. Dream interpretation can outline what issues a person may be dealing with or may explore different parts of a person not yet in consciousness. Many theorists have explored dreams in conjunction with psychotherapy. I use dreams with clients who are not in touch with what they're feeling. My clients think their dreams are fascinating and that they reveal inner thoughts and desires.

A part of Shame wanted to ask Love for help, and her dream was about a part of herself leading her to call on Light. This part was very strong but was not known to Shame in everyday life. We can program our subconscious mind to focus on the light instead of darkness, the positive instead of negative, the opportunities instead of failure.

The experience of recovery opens us up as human beings, connects us with our true self—our higher self—and aligns us with light. We can throw off the shame and darkness and join the happy people living an authentic life. It's a paradise only because we have the presence of a loving entity inside us we never knew existed. We may have believed in our minds, but recovery puts us in touch with and connects us to joy and expands our realm of possibilities.

We must explore those parts of ourselves we're unfamiliar with. Being inside the village of Patience can be a process of rebirth. Admission into a spiritual community based on the 12-step lifestyle is open to everyone. Of course we want to skip steps or speed up the process. Recovery requires faith, hope, and surrender. This means we need to turn our will and our life over to God as we understand him. Many people are afraid of recovery because they feel undeserving of light and love.

Everyone in a spiritual community is reaching out for the strength and power they can never get alone. It's the power of the group that brings the strength, just as much as prayer and meditation do. A spiritual community is like the city of Patience, where love and understanding replace violence and self-abusing thoughts and behaviors.

By living in the light, we're able to face the dawn and feel the warmth of the sunrise beating down on us. Light is now pleasant, healthy, and renewing. The group is a safe haven and you will feel nurtured and cared for. This may take either a long time or a short time, depending on your level of trust and if you can relinquish control.

Our loving part reprograms and reparents us. A newborn trusts that his or her parents will love unconditionally. Unconditional love is the key to the program. Many of us can't accept ourselves if we're less than perfect. Embracing a spiritual lifestyle brings hope to those who have tried and failed at doing it alone. We can grieve for our losses and share our pain at meetings with others who can understand. This is the gift of belonging.

Ask yourself the following questions to see how open you are to the spiritual process and the power that lies within you. After you have answered the questions, go back and read the story again. This will give you some insight into your fears, obstacles, and feelings regarding spirituality and recovery.

Questions for Discussion:

1. Can you link your intellect with your emotions, or do they operate separately? How do you make decisions? Do you use your head, gut, or a combination of the two?
2. Do you sometimes hide from the truth of who you are inside?
3. Do you have a hard time remembering your dreams?
4. How do you feel about other people bringing you wisdom or the will of a higher power? Would you trust that other people could help you in this path?

5. How do you feel about power? Does power come from a higher power or a higher part of ourselves? Can power be used to help others as well?
6. What do you think kept Shame in the dark? Do you enjoy the darkness because it is known?
7. Would you have trusted what Love was saying to Shame? Would you test Love to see if what he was saying was accurate, or would you take a leap of faith?
8. How do you feel about light? Does light frighten you? What would others see if they put the spotlight on you?
9. What did you think of the Queen's message to Shame at the end of the story? Would you be able to carry out these instructions? Why or why not?
10. Did you understand why "making mistakes and being human" was the password to the recovery road? What other passwords could fit?
11. What do you think would be the hardest part of getting on the recovery road?
12. What do you think would be the easiest part? Would you take the risk? Why?

6

Exploring Life's Meaning and the 12-Step Program

As a society we have strayed from using our innate sense of intuition and our River Within. There's a big movement in this country to return to our spiritual roots so we can find more meaning and purpose in our lives. Acquiring more toys and material goods is not fulfilling to us. Society is guiding us toward workaholism. While we were on vacation in Michigan, the priest at Sunday mass had to remind parishioners to rest on Sunday. He kept reminding us we needed rest on a regular basis.

People are working much more than ever but the trappings of success leave them empty and searching. They wonder "Is this all there is?" Not only must we continue to think about what is meaningful to us, we need to return to nature and the quiet necessary for inner peace. No one ever told us there was value in exploring our inner self and the world around us. We get so busy, we forget our spiritual life.

I recently saw the movie *Grand Canyon.* It spoke to spiritual issues and explored some of life's broader questions about whether or not events in our life happen for a reason.

These questions have been around for a long time. What is our purpose? What's the meaning of life? Why are we drawn to certain things or places? Are we being led to a better life, or do we have control over everything in our lives? This is a common struggle no matter how much recovery a person has.

In *Grand Canyon*, Kevin Kline's character meets Danny Glover's character when Kline's character is stranded in a gang-infested neighborhood and is about to be robbed by gang members. Glover's character, arriving in tow truck, manages to save Kline's character from being harmed. Kline's character begins to ask himself the meaning of the event, and thinks back to another time in his life when he was saved from harm. The first time he was saved, he didn't get a chance to speak to the woman who helped him and really thank her. He decides to visit Glover's character the next day and takes him out to breakfast.

He feels some sort of connection to Glover but doesn't know why. How many of us struggle with the same feelings? In the movie, this one meeting affected many people's lives. The theme of black people and white people working together is also a spiritual one. Since that incident in the basement, I knew I had a destiny that involved telling my story. I've had many coincidences that really were the result of divine intervention. When I call on God, I get an answer.

Once, I was speaking to a client who works with cancer patients. She told me that patients from all different backgrounds start forming connections they never would have made before their illness. Isn't it sad that we need to have cancer or a terminal illness to learn how to accept others? For one thing, pain and suffering is universal. We all know what pain is. It would be beneficial to the world if we shared more of our pain with each other.

I recently asked God to let me know if I was really meant to be a writer. He answered through a card I received a few days later from a friend and colleague. The card stated that she read a story I had written in my last newsletter. She told me I was a talented writer. I almost fell over—I had received my answer.

I read in the March 29, 1992, issue of the *Chicago Tribune* that according to a survey, 36 percent of the population believes they have spoken to God. I decided to share all of my spiritual stories to let you know that if you speak to God, you're not crazy. My guess is this percentage is much higher but people are afraid to admit it. People are also afraid their experiences are less important or dramatic. Experiences are subtle or direct; each kind is just as important. I also was afraid but can no longer hide my spiritual self. Allow your spiritual self to come out and share.

Religious leaders also claim they have spoken with God. Recently, I was at a Eucharistic Ministers Training Program. One of the speakers was talking about a time when he asked God for a sign and was given what he asked for. He also asked if we felt we were called to serve God in any way. Ask yourself that question. Were you compelled to do something you thought God had asked you to do? In *Grand Canyon*, Kline's character's wife was jogging and found a baby hidden in the bushes. She wanted to adopt the child because she thought God or a higher being had allowed her to find the child for some reason unknown to her.

In her book *Return to Love*, Marianne Williamson talks about the way little children know how to love. As we mature, we lose this ability and start to believe and live in a fearful way. Her book speaks to the need for surrendering one's life to a higher power. This way we can be guided back to love. She also claims God was gentle with her, not punishing. I've found this to be true as well. My clients speak every day about the miracles and spiritual connections they've experienced. Think about what I'm saying; yes, it's frightening to hear God's voice, but once you do, you'll want more of the love and comfort you have received.

Spiritual Growth and 12-Step Program Summary of Steps

Spiritual development helps us look inward for our strength and connect to a greater good that accepts us unconditionally. A 12-step program is a commitment to honesty and a healthy environment wherein changes and miracles take place.

We live in a shame-based society. People feel flawed or defective and feel as if they're "a mistake." There are two kinds of shame. Healthy shame helps us understand that we have limits and are human. It begins when we're about fifteen months old. The need to balance shame and doubt with autonomy is a primary developmental task. In dysfunctional families, many healthy behaviors have shame attached to them.

This is toxic shame. Toxic shame is a dark, powerful feeling that tells us we're a mistake, or that it's wrong to ask for what we want. Parents shame the child because they don't know how to meet the child's need for having fun, giving love, or honest communication. The current literature on shame suggests it is much easier to shame a child into conformity than to admit lack of parenting skills.

Healthy shame turns to toxic shame when the emotion becomes a state of being and is internalized. Toxic shame cuts us off from our drives, instincts, and humanness. Toxic shame binds the person, and the person turns to mood altering all feelings and hides from himself and the world.

Any emotion can be healthy or toxic. Healthy guilt is when we make a mistake and feel remorse about it. Toxic guilt is when we don't make a mistake but feel as if we did. In other words, we take on other people's mistakes and blame ourselves. Toxic guilt and shame are the focus in a recovery program. Toxic emotions are obstacles to the spiritual process. Some people don't feel worthy enough to be loved unconditionally by God.

Do we have respect for ourselves and others, or do we criticize, gossip, and talk behind their backs? Do we see ourselves as different from other people? The only way we can move from a shame-based society into a respect-based society is to:

1. Accept all of ourselves and all of others.
2. Break codependent patterns.
3. Reconnect to a higher power and our spiritual self.
4. Develop more compassion for ourselves, others, and nature.
5. Use abundance and prosperity principles.

When we're addicted to another person, substance, or activity, we are detaching from God or a higher power. We don't need him because we believe we must have all the answers to heal ourselves. This is called insanity or distorted thinking. Recovery begins when we start to realize we can no longer do it alone. People admit they're helpless and need a power outside themselves to begin healing. People need a safe place to talk where others can understand their pain and feelings.

For many years, I was so depressed I could hardly stand to live so I put walls around this depression. When I was tired of feeling sorry for myself, I would get angry and push forward with my career. I would use anything to focus on. Of course I never got anything but exhausted from this behavior. However, that was the only way I knew of to help me get out of my depression. Just to clear my head, I would exercise for hours since I was often confused and couldn't concentrate.

Each year around autumn I had a clinical depression. The symptoms were cloudy thinking, lack of motivation, fatigue, and crying. After the New Year, I'd start to feel better. However, I hid this from everyone by being manic and by avoiding close friendships. I always cried alone.

This seasonal depression started when I was eight years old. My mother had a nervous breakdown in front of me and I never forgot the pain of seeing her crying, slumped on the floor, begging me not to leave her alone. I was so scared and depressed that all I could focus on was food.

When I entered a 12-step meeting for the first time, people were breaking down and crying. That made me very nervous and uncomfortable, because I'd never allowed anyone to see me cry except my mother and my neighbor, Cindy. I finally chose to share my grief with others and ask for God's help. I let down the walls. When I was able to share with my group members, I found belonging and acceptance I'd never imagined.

Do you want to focus on what strengths you have, or do you want to look at what you don't have? Do you want to stop struggling and exhausting yourself? We can choose to be honest with ourselves and see our humanness. When I finally spoke about my depression at my ACOA meeting, people related to it and thanked me. I thought they would reject me and be mad because I expressed my feelings. To get a different outcome than in the past, I had to take the risk.

In a respect-based society, we all need each other. With spiritual development, we can experience all of our emotions, accept them, and feel as if we are never alone. Spiritual development has helped me to be more kind and nurturing both to myself and to others. I use my group as a cheering section and often visualize them during the week. They are like the family I never had. My other choice was to stay in my shame-based prison which offered me perfectionism and the ability to hide my true self. In my shame-based world there was always something wrong with me, and I had no healthy relationships. By adding spirituality to my life, I've a new-found freedom and confidence I didn't have before. I have self-respect, health, and a thriving business and personal life.

Spiritual Development Will Help You To:

1. Reach your potential as a human being—create meaning and purpose.
2. Raise your self-esteem by taking small risks to self-disclose.
3. Focus on the positive points and develop serenity and peace.
4. Let go of old, angry resentments and start forgiving yourself and others.
5. Break the chains of victimization and bondage.

6. Learn self-acceptance and how to protect yourself.
7. Decrease your stress level.
8. Tap into your intuitive power and your extra-ordinary talents and skills.

Spiritual development is the birthright of everyone. We can be who we are and reach our potential as human beings. If we live a spiritual or inner life, we realize that we live by certain values, believe in The River Within, and believe God is inside us.

If the above statement frightens you, it may be because religion and some of its doctrines have suggested that God is a punishing God. My Catholic clients talk most about being afraid of punishment. Some believe if they even think something "bad," it's a sin. Others believe they can never be angry at God or a man of the cloth. The way your parents talked about God is probably ingrained in you.

If your parents used God to put fear in you, it will be hard to trust God to bring only what is in your best interests. Think about the way your parents dealt with God. What were the family rituals around religion and holidays? Were you obligated to go to church? Did you go to church in shifts or at the same time each week? Take some time to think about your beliefs regarding God, the church, and religion.

Spirituality is different from religion but most people think they are the same. Spirituality is a way of life, whereas religion is a set of rules or an organized set of principles. We don't have to attend church to be considered spiritual.

Spirituality helps us learn how to respect ourselves, others, nature, and find inner peace. Having a relationship and dialogue with God in a 12-step or spiritual program is more direct than in religion. There is no priest, rabbi, or minister between you and God. You can communicate with him or her directly.

Living an outer, external life, means looking outside ourselves for approval, identity, and validation. In this type of life, we feel drained, used, manipulated, and too dependent on others for our good feelings. We don't allow ourselves to believe in or use The River Within.

I can tell you that the external life is much more stressful and unmanageable than the inner life. However, the process of going from an outer life to an inner life takes risk, hard work, and a reconnection with God. We can create our own life and don't need to be chained to the will or opinions of others for our self-esteem.

I work with many people who have eating disorders. Some of my clients make the scale powerful—weighing their self-esteem. If they weigh 120, they're good. If they weigh 122, they're bad. They give power to the scale itself and rely on the scale to tell them if they are a "good" person or a "bad" person. If you didn't know these people are slaves to the scale, you'd be shocked to hear they give a scale so much power over their lives.

Codependent people make other people their Gods, and rely on others to define them and tell them who they are and what they need to do. They haven't developed good boundaries. Many people don't know where they begin and where they end. They don't know how to look in the mirror and give themselves affirmations or call on God for help.

So many families are enmeshed. Enmeshment means family members don't each have a separate identity. Family members believe they can feel another family member's pain. When someone from the family tries to have a separate identity, the family often reacts with anger and feels as if they're being betrayed. This disloyal person is often abandoned emotionally and/or physically for his or her transgressions. This is extremely painful. In dysfunctional families, the family doesn't promote or value independence and leaving home.

Many times children and parents reconnect after a time when the adult child forms boundaries and an identity of his or her own. During the process of separation and individuation, a person may decide to limit contact or have no contact at all with his or her family. These are very hard choices people often make in recovery.

In 12-step meetings, I've heard how upset a brother or sister is over a divorce or incident in their siblings' lives. The person speaking has no idea what's going on within themselves, so they focus on what's wrong with other family members. I have clients who believe that even when they're adults they still need to mediate their parents' fights and conflicts. This is more prevalent than we think. It's so hard to break old roles, patterns, and habits. Some adult children still believe they're responsible for fixing family problems and/or protecting one of their parents against the other.

People have the right to separate and be themselves. This is how we begin a spiritual journey. Our lives are our own. No one can spare us from pain; nor can we spare others from pain. We can't control other people. If we try, we lose ourselves in the process. Focus on your own plan and goals—this is the way to serenity.

The Twelve Steps in Perspective

Step 1: *We admitted we were powerless over the effects of addiction and our lives had become unmanageable.*

This step is the first step toward a spiritual life. Many of us believe if we understand ourselves our addiction will be cured. We think we have the answer to everything. In choosing to work this step, we're finally trying to reconnect with God by admitting we are powerless and can't do it alone. In a sense, we're laying the foundation for our recovery. I realized I was unable to change the circumstances of my life; therefore I needed help from another source. Whatever I tried wasn't working—and the things that had worked in the past weren't giving me the relief they once had.

Most people have a hard time admitting helplessness because it suggests failure or defeat in some way. Many people think only about the good times of the addiction and tend to forget the negative or painful consequences. This is the most gentle and calming step, since it frees us from being isolated and alone.

Step 2: *Came to believe that a power greater than ourselves could restore us to sanity.*

A variation on this step speaks about restoring us to wholeness rather than sanity. Remember, insanity is the distorted thinking that is part of the addiction. When you review the behavior and activities of someone while they are under the influence or in a crisis, it looks as if they are insane. What we're hoping to achieve is a life in which we can accept all of ourselves and all of others. This is wholeness. This step provides hope for a happy life that may seem impossible to fathom from the depths of addiction or despair.

Belief in a higher power is not a magical cure. Some people find it hard to believe in a merciful and kind God. However, a shift in perception is a miracle.

Step 3: *Made a decision to turn our will and our lives over to the care of God as we understand him.*

This step is calling us to action. We need to admit our neediness and make a commitment to a higher power we can't see. We're saying we need God in our lives. This is extremely frightening for everyone.

Anyone who has been ritualistically abused or sexually/physically abused has much fear. I urge you to seek counseling. I was confused about who God was. Was he a good force or an evil force? Remember that God is not an actual man or woman.

Step 4: *Made a searching and fearless moral inventory of ourselves.*

A client of mine was in recovery for a drug and alcohol problem. He would not do a 4th step inventory. I asked him why. He replied he didn't want to get in touch with his "old using" self. He only wanted to focus on who he was today. This is one of the hardest steps to do because it asks us to be honest about who we are and where we came from. We need to look at our roots, childhood hurts and actions, depression, approval seeking, and loneliness. Perhaps we find that when we look at ourselves, we see things we don't like. This step asks us to come out of hiding, to get to know ourselves.

For so many of us, it's easier to know others than it is to know ourselves. We need to explore the hidden, darker parts of ourselves that we've locked away. This step is essential for reaching wholeness. With increased awareness of who we are, we can change old behaviors and feelings. We can accept the dark or hidden parts as human.

Step 5: *Admitted to God, to ourselves, and to another human being the exact nature of our wrongs.*

This step requires honesty and reconciliation with God. Reconciliation is the process of harmonizing things that are opposed and inconsistent. Step 5 is difficult and tends to be avoided because it asks us to tell our story to another person. We are asked to be vulnerable, which is not an easy task. I went to my priest and asked for forgiveness. I realized I was holding myself responsible for my father's sins and was confessing for him. The priest blessed me, forgave me, and told me to go and be a happy girl. For many years, I protected my father's secret and sins. It was new not to have to protect him and the secret anymore.

After doing this step, I felt connected to God again, even if I didn't understand his logic. This was my pathway out of isolation and keeping my father's secrets. It was like a baptism. Other people or clients have spoken to friends or other professionals for their 5th step. I urge anyone in the program to complete this step. It set me free from years of self-punishment, self-hatred, and guilt.

Step 6: *Were entirely ready to have God remove these defects of character.*

Step 6 and 7 ask us to deal directly with God. In this step we are asked to be entirely ready. We need to surrender again. For this we need to do what it takes to ask for his help. The concepts of rest and waiting are hard for most of us who grew up in dysfunctional families. However, that's what we must do in step 6. Faith and patience are needed.

Step 7: *Humbly asked him to remove our shortcomings.*

To complete this step, we must develop and practice humility—the only way to achieve peace, serenity, and happiness. We may not want to release some of our old familiar patterns even if they are unhealthy. Recently, a client told me it was easier to stick with the old devils than trade them in for angels. Depressed clients say the same thing. Why get rid of something that is so comfortable? This step asks us to deal with the letting go process which involves loss, risk, grief, and change. In this step we need the strength to believe life will be better if some traits are let go.

Letting go can be a very threatening thing. Many believe nothing will come and they will be empty. I tell them something always comes out of nothing. This is the surprise and the celebration part of step 7. Many clients feel they're betraying their families if they get too healthy. This is a valid point and one reason why some people resist positive change. In order for this step to be completed, we must do whatever footwork is needed. God does not wave a magic wand over us to take away our defects. We need to fear less and believe more.

Step 8: *Made a list of all persons we had harmed and became willing to make amends to them all.*

Think of step 8 as dealing with resentment, both for ourselves and for others. Most of my clients have harmed themselves much more than they've harmed others. This is often a painful discovery. When people realize how vicious and nasty they've been to themselves, they can't seem to believe it. This step emphasizes the possibility for change and greater self-acceptance. The concept of healthy guilt and penance apply here as well. We must realize and take responsibility for our behavior, past and present. Healthy guilt is when you admit making a mistake and apologize. Step 8 is also a lesson in integrity and honesty. Willingness is the key word. Keeping all of this locked inside restricts the amount of space for growth, so a good housecleaning is needed in this step. (Love God, Clean House, Help Others)

Step 9: *Made direct amends to such people whenever possible, except when to do so would injure them or others.*

We need to be cautious taking this action step. It helps rebuild self-esteem by making us aware of our part in the difficulty of our relationships. The forgiveness process needs to be applied here, toward oneself and others. Consider a butterfly emerging from its cocoon. If we try to push the process and open the cocoon before its time, the butterfly dies. The truth is—we can't skip steps or rush the process.

This step brings an opportunity to redefine relationships, accept the consequences of our behavior, and take responsibility for any new insights that may emerge. Don't be afraid of hurting someone when you make amends. The truth will help both of you and enable you to be on different ground after amends have been made. The fear of hurting another person and procrastination are the main obstacles to completing this step.

Don't confuse step 9 with making an apology. An apology is when we regret our behavior and say we're sorry. Making amends requires us to change or alter our behavior. Expressing regret for having done something incorrect is not enough.

One client sent a check to a grocery store anonymously to pay for the food she stole while shopping there. She was making amends. Other people have presented a check in person. How you do it is up to you. In step 9, we're asked to put aside our prior distractions and obsessions and focus on forgiveness. This step involves much personal courage and the ability to be vulnerable.

When might it be appropriate to not make amends? For example, if you were in a violent, abusive, or codependent relationship, you might not want to reconnect with an unsafe person. If a person is unstable either physically or mentally, it might not be a good idea to make amends. It's better to make amends indirectly.

One of my clients has been very mean and insensitive to an old boyfriend. However, this was a very unhealthy codependent relationship that took her years to break away from. Since she had known this man in college, she made a donation to the school and wrote a letter of apology to him but didn't mail it. Some people can't handle the emotional consequences of a person telling them a secret they might have repressed or been unaware of.

For those who are divorced and had an affair during their marriage, it might be better to deal with making amends in an indirect way. We need to be very careful when making amends. If there is any doubt about this issue, please consult a trusted counselor, friend, or clergy member.

I believe the person we've harmed most often is ourselves. In step 9, it's a good idea to look at the damage you have done to yourself. Many of my clients come to this revelation while doing this step. The forgiveness process begins and we stop blaming others for our mistakes and traumas. This process also applies when someone stops hurting themselves for what others may have done. To make amends to yourself is to begin to repair your sense of value and self-respect. One way to do this is to write an amends letter to yourself, outlining all the things you've done to injure, sabotage, restrict, or punish yourself. This is a very freeing thing to do.

Step 10: *Continued to take personal inventory and when we were wrong promptly admitted it.*

We are reminded of our commitment in this step. We can no longer risk inappropriate behavior or unhealthy attitudes and need to be aware of red flags signaling our past resentments or fears. I know when I start judging others, worrying obsessively, or missing meetings, I need to take a look at my feelings. This step acknowledges who we are today. There is an abundance of help for those who admit their mistakes. For some, mistakes are often treated like a crime. In this step, mistakes are merely a learning experience.

Step 10 reminds us we need to maintain the program on a daily basis. Remember, we never finish the program. Many of us get tired of the program or mistake feeling better about ourselves with finishing our work. A client told me she wished the steps would work so she'd be home free. It doesn't work like that. Danger signals of slipping away from the program include anxiety, irritability, and extreme frustration. Missing meetings becomes a habit. In reality we can no longer afford ineffective behaviors. We need continued and ongoing spiritual development.

This is a very freeing step because it focuses us on our own behavior. For many of my clients people-pleasing, approval-seeking, and self-defeating thoughts and behaviors continue to be issues. I remind them of the price of being nice. It's usually the clients forgetting about this step who continue to feel physically and emotionally drained. Some continue comparing themselves to others and believe they're a failure.

One client constantly undermines her new-found self-acceptance and victimizes herself by going back into the past and focusing on all of her mistakes. She focuses on men who have left her, describes herself as a loser, and is ashamed of her past dependency issues in these relationships. Often, I speak of how her mother modeled codependent behavior and how her parents divorce was very painful for her. Her father was an alcoholic who wasn't there emotionally for her.

I help her to separate the codependent issues, the past, and her currently healthy relationship with her husband. We talk about mistakes and what she learned from early relationships with men. Accepting her mistakes and grieving for old losses helps her to be open to new ways of relating and self-acceptance.

Like many of my clients, we need to know that giving our power to men or women and feeling like all break-ups were our fault is self-abusive and ineffective. It brings us back to self-defeating thinking and allows us to look only at our flaws, not relationship issues. We talk about how unmet childhood needs for love create adult relationship issues and poor choices. Being aware of old patterns and ineffective thinking helps us by offering an opportunity to see ourselves and our past mistakes in a more positive and forgiving light.

Self-care is always the first thing to slip away and we must bring it back into focus. Creating an atmosphere of routine self-inventories and check-ins helps in this regard. Ask yourself, "Did I do anything to take care of myself this week?" Many times, a daily or weekly review can help with this step.

Step 11: *Sought through prayer and meditation to improve our conscious contact with God as we understood him, praying only for the knowledge of his will for us and the power to carry it out.*

In this step, we are deepening our partnership with God that we started in steps 2 and 3. God's will for us will be revealed, although this often provokes anxiety. Step 11 continues leading us down the path to acknowledge our plan and purpose in this world. I call it "the mission in motion." It calls for quiet meditation time, prayer, faith, and persistence. Meditation is the ancient practice that can calm the mind. Like any art, it takes practice and persistence to develop. The hardest thing in this step is to avoid trying to control outcomes. There are books on how to meditate and these might be helpful. Yoga is another way to quiet the mind and heal the body.

How many of us have tried to ask God only for what we wanted? It's really difficult to fully trust that God's will can benefit you—especially if you're being tested or faced with a dilemma. My friend Jan explained step 11 this way: You are a mouse in a cage. You see a piece of cheese outside your cage but don't see the cat waiting for you behind the chair. You're upset because you want the cheese and can't figure out why you can't have it. How many of us can see the obstacles that seem to be so far away? Even though there's a reason God won't let you get the cheese, you don't know why. It takes a strong faith to remember God is protecting us and keeping us safe for our own good.

Step 12: *Having had a spiritual awakening as a result of these steps, we tried to carry this message to others and to practice these principles in all our affairs.*

In step 12 we watch as darkness turns to light. We notice a shift in our value system. This step emphasizes new awareness, insights, or feelings once foreign to us—love, joy, happiness, and peacefulness. This is not the end, but a rebirth of our commitment to the realm of the spirit. Spiritual growth is not a distinct event with a clear beginning and ending. We are continuing to evolve and grow throughout our life. We're always "becoming" and reaching for more compassion, love, and serenity. Service to the community is the way in which we bring the program to others—either by our example or by our stories.

A spiritual awakening is not like the Fourth of July, with fireworks and noise. Often an awakening is a new insight, feeling, or thought. An awakening is not sudden. We are continually awakening, planting, and harvesting throughout our lives. One thing that remains is the humility and the power of our program. We touch others with the love and openness God has touched us with, and we try to see the good in others. If we see the good in others, we increase love and decrease fear in our lives. Let's share our gift with others. The spirit in you perceives the spirit in others.

7

Help for Old Habits

When depressed, I thought of myself as a victim with no power to change my lot in life. Believing I was destined to marry an alcoholic and be miserable for the rest of my life, I wanted to change my lifescript. We all have the capacity to change. History is not destiny.

I had to begin to emotionally withdraw from my family of origin, take risks, get out on my own, and look at myself in the mirror for affirmation and praise. I looked to my higher power for answers and prayed that all would work out for me. Miracles can happen and I wanted my share! This was no easy task. Growing up was the hardest thing I ever did in my life. It's one of my most important and powerful achievements as well.

Before this, I was looking to please others to gain approval. Just to hear my boss say, "That was really great," I went so far as to work until exhaustion. Of course he never said that enough, no matter what I did. I kept working and struggling, working and struggling. I was addicted to urgency and couldn't seem to get out of the pattern. Convinced I could do it on my own without help, I almost killed myself with self-abusive thoughts and behavior. I never said, "I'm lost, help me." This was my strength—I thought. Although my stomach hurt and it felt as if a rock was stuck in there, I pretended all was well.

My justification for going to therapy was that I could *pay* for help. This made me feel better about being needy. I was missing something essential—my own sense of individuality, self-love, value, and power. Until I was able to surrender to a higher power and ask for help, I couldn't change. I had to be humble. The foundation of the 12-step program is to attain humility. The steps test our humility. The more humility we have, the greater compassion and self-acceptance we have.

Calling on God was the beginning of my healing and recovery. You can do the same right now. I had to learn to give up the masks I used and realize I was human. My compulsive behavior was my hunger, but it wasn't for food. Food could not fill the type of hunger I had. Only God or the higher power could fill my emptiness and my hunger. I had to be honest about the deficits, voids, and holes inside me.

I like the way God is teaching me to take care of myself and see myself as a priority. Before, I would rearrange my schedule to accommodate others. Now, I want to live my own life, not someone else's.

I needed balance in my life. Everyone needs to balance their lives. If you're spending too much time on social or intellectual pursuits, you're taking time and energy away from other areas that also need attention. Of course, no one is perfect, but for harmony to exist we must tend to our spiritual side. This is the most overlooked part.

We need to have intellectual, social, emotional, physical, and spiritual parts to our life. People were meant to be one with themselves and the universe. Individual growth is not valued in our society. Many believe they are selfish if they like themselves or if they give themselves a pat on the back. This is an obstacle to spiritual growth. Some of my clients also believe if they do something that doesn't produce or lead to money, it's a waste of time. Self-care, recreation, and the self have no value unless one is working or producing. How many of us have lived our lives on a treadmill, trying to produce more in less time? This is counter to a spiritual life, which focuses on balance, wholeness, and compassion for others.

Living in our dysfunctional homes, we had distorted views of ourselves and the world around us. With no sense of identity and no boundaries, we allowed other people, activities, or substances to take control of our lives. We were stuck in depressive or codependent patterns which further caused a sense of self-loathing and insignificance. Our attitudes, beliefs, and values may have set us up for abandonment or pain, but we continued on—unaware. We didn't learn decision-making and interpersonal skills or discover our healthy limitations. We can't see how our character defects hurt us. Our wounded inner child influences our current behavior and actions without our conscious knowledge. The program, however, brings the pain to the surface, heals the pain, and reparents the inner child.

The 12-step program, like therapy, can teach you these skills and encourage you to look inward in a fearless and honest way. The program helps you get honest—out of denial. Remember, you can only change something about yourself if you come to know and accept it first. Denial is unconscious. You don't even know you're in it. Denial is a powerful defense that keeps you from becoming overwhelmed with the dysfunctional concerns. Therefore, when a painful childhood memory is awakened, we feel exactly like we did as a child, even if we were able to numb the pain at the time.

This feeling is met with fear and out-of-control behavior. In therapy, what I do with people is hook up their intellect with their emotions. This allows people to understand that intellectually they may be twenty-seven or whatever adult age they are, but their emotions are childlike and much younger. This is how people grow in therapy.

The adult part attempts to teach the inner child new coping skills. This is a healthy process, but very anxiety-producing and disturbing. The 12-step program and therapy can work together to bring to the surface and integrate parts of you that are younger, hurt, angry, or sad.

As you go though the 12-step process, you're able to be more conscious and reflective. This is an example of a spiritual awakening. The awakening is sometimes a new feeling, insight, or thought that causes a shift in your perception of yourself and the world. The awakening process helps the therapist point out old patterns, feelings that have been stifled, and continue the process of reparenting.

Many adult children have stopped growing at certain developmental stages; the goal is to go back to those places, heal the wounds, and move them along to the next phase. Besides helping people function adequately in the present, we need to do this work on the past. This process helps teach us how to accept reality and how to learn new coping skills.

In therapy, the goal is to uncover the family of origin issues, learn what you want to keep and discard, and to build self-esteem and a sense of self-worth. I want to commend anyone who is in a 12-step program and engaging in therapy at the same time. You are truly courageous and strong. Try to give yourself credit for all the things you are doing to accept help, humility, and the therapeutic process.

Let me be honest about the work of therapy. It takes a tremendous amount of commitment, trust, and faith to gain from a therapeutic relationship. Hopefully, your therapist will talk to you about the relationship between the two of you, which is the most important part of therapy for adult children. The therapist needs to be supportive, understanding, and knowledgeable about how the 12-step program works.

The therapist you choose might share personal life experiences or training, making you feel as if he or she could be empathic to your situation. You need to feel safe with the therapist. If you don't feel right about your counselor, don't be afraid to ask questions about his or her skills and training. You have a right to the kind of professional you need. After a month or two in therapy, if you don't feel understood or heard, tell the therapist your feelings. Don't be afraid to tell the therapist if you are angry for any reason.

Many clients I work with are most afraid of acknowledging just how dysfunctional their family background is. This is a common feeling. Also, many are afraid of spiritual development, and associate it with voodoo, new age, or satanic cults. I can understand the fear, because we all have a fear of the unknown. However, believe me when I say the 12-step program can be a wonderful place to grow.

The 12-steps are worked in order but may be repeated. When a person stops working the program, or begins to miss meetings, we call this relapse. A relapse is just that—a break in the program. No recovery is without relapse. Relapses teach us to look at certain obstacles or any resistance we have toward growing and changing. Working the steps can never be a perfect or totally smooth progression. However, when we relapse, we never go back to square one again. We simply do the next right thing and forgive ourselves.

Spirituality allows us to find out who we really are and points us toward a healthy, happy life. To be spiritual, a person must have some self-esteem. Using principles from the program enables us to find a new source of energy and zest. Spiritual people are living—not merely surviving. How many of us lead a dead life? A spiritual life puts us directly into a relationship with God or the higher power. We don't need to go to church to find him. However, choosing to go to church will not work against developing a spiritual life.

Recovery starts when we begin to change our beliefs, feelings, and attitudes and build a new way of living. The 12-step program and therapy help us uncover and discover the benefits of a spiritual life. By expanding our spiritual life, we move toward a sense of peace, love, and serenity. When we practice the principles of the program, we're blessed with miracles and a sense of purpose we may not have felt before embarking on the journey. The steps can be worked at our own pace or we can join a step group to go over the steps one by one.

Twelve-step meetings are places where we can go to find other people who share something. Those who grew up in alcoholic, dysfunctional homes can relate to each other's pain and confusion. Overeaters and alcoholics can find comfort and fellowship with others on the same road to recovery. By attending meetings and working the steps, we can communicate with the higher power. We can have a partnership with a higher power to help us meet our goals and help us reach our true potential as a human being.

A sponsor is a 12-step member who is willing to work with another person toward spiritual development and understanding the program. The sponsor is not a therapist and doesn't get paid. While helping another person grow and learn, a sponsor learns much about himself or herself. He or she usually has at least a few years of experience in a recovery program.

The program helps us share our strength, hope, and experiences with others. The concept of giving back is integral in the 12-step program. This is where we speak to a group or help a newcomer understand the program. When we have gratitude for the program, we try to give something back to the 12-step community, which acts like a healthy family.

In meetings, if you're talking in a small group, no one is allowed to interrupt. This helps others listen without being able to jump in. Many times family members talk all at once. In a meeting, you're free to speak as long as you need on a topic. You're allowed to have your own opinions and thoughts. Usually there's a speaker who picks a relevant topic for discussion. It could be about a common trait, a personal difficulty with some aspect of the program, or a certain step. I urge you to go to a 12-step meeting and see for yourself the power of these self-help groups.

What will happen when we develop spirituality? Joe Klass, in his book, *The 12 Steps to Happiness*, explains that God can manage our lives better than we can. This helps us believe more in our intuition and ourselves. Klass believes, as do I, that spiritual development and the 12-steps will work for anybody and everybody.

I would urge you to take a spiritual development class, workshop, or read recovery material. I conduct workshops and classes in this regard. Something inside you urged you to read this book. Trust your inner voice on this one!

Obstacles to the 12-Step Process:

1. Seeing God as a punishing God
2. Control and the illusion of control (ACOA especially)
3. Perfectionism
4. Anger and resentments
5. Unwilling to surrender to the "letting go" process
6. Pride and ego
7. Resistance to the positive process

Obstacles for Continued Reliance on a 12-Step Program:

1. Not seeing relapse as part of the program
2. Testing to see if one is really addicted
3. Impatience (I want it done my way)
4. Not acknowledging that God is a resource for you
5. Inability or fear of doing 4th step work
6. Problem with sponsors (some don't believe therapy is necessary)
7. Fear of showing emotion at meetings
8. Rescuing behavior or dating other members of the 12-step group

9. Thinking one is "cured" and can stop going to meetings

Some Common Misconceptions of a 12-Step Program:

1. I'm cured and can stop going to meetings soon.
2. The program will work by itself and I don't have to do anything.
3. My 12-step journey will be painless and easy.
4. The program is so overwhelming. I can't possibly keep up.
5. The program will fix all of my defects and take away my flaws.
6. I can go through the 12-step book by myself. I don't need meetings.
7. A single external event will give me a spiritual awakening.
8. I know how the program works and can tell you the complete process.
9. I know the higher power doesn't have time for my small problems.
10. I have my therapist and she/he is my higher power.
11. If I do much service work, I can get what I want from God.
12. If I am confused about how the program works, I'm not getting it.

Tips on How to Understand These Myths and Misconceptions:

1. No one really knows how the 12-step program works, so don't try to analyze it.
2. Share your confusion. It's not a bad feeling—deal with the lack of control issue.
3. Allow yourself to talk about fears, shame, anger, and resentments.
4. The higher power doesn't make deals, but miracles can happen.
5. Speak to issues that might block you from accepting the goodness within you.
6. We are powerless over other people and their addictions.

Exercises in Spiritual Development:

1. Higher Power—many people are frightened by the notion of a higher power. Here are some exercises to strengthen contact. (HP=higher power)
    a. Envision the higher power as a beautiful man or woman. Smile at the HP. Ask the HP a question. Remember, the HP is life giving. Put a bubble around yourself and visualize the HP filling the bubble with white light. Bask in the light.
    b. Visualize a bright yellow sun shining down from the heavens onto a flower that's just budding. Imagine the flower blooming as the light shines on it.

2. Higher Self or Intuition—many people don't think they have a highly evolved part of themselves that is a guide who knows what's best for them. Many times the gut tells us to do things but we don't listen. Intuition develops when we value the information it provides us with.
   a. Visualize a part of you that is connected to God. It could be a silver thread or a string. The connection can come from your head, heart, or emotions. Allow the higher self to ask the higher power for guidance. Visualize your hands outstretched toward the sky and yellow light flowing to you from the sky. Repeat the following: There is a part of me that knows what I need to do.
   b. Have a book of hunches so you can record what your gut is asking you to do. Go somewhere quiet and listen to any messages from your mind or emotions.
   c. Visualize yourself fully healed. What do you look like? Paste together or draw a picture of this and put it somewhere you can see. Put living things around you and include nature in the scenario.

8

Messages from the Deep Self: Shelter in the Forest

From time to time, I've received very enlightening messages that will help you understand you don't have to be afraid of listening to your inner voice. When I first started to meditate, I heard, "You seek wisdom through the mind, you do not use your heart. Tap into the deadness in your heart and you will fly to another plane."

I've always felt a heavy burden in my heart that came from all my negative experiences, but I had never thought about using my heart. This higher plane of thinking helped me have more compassion for my own heartache. I created my speaking program, "Speaking From the Heart," for exactly those reasons. To deal with my heartache, I had to reconnect to my family of origin. My meditations kept urging me to reconnect. The image I received was of two telephone poles with the lines down being reconnected.

Why did I reconnect with my mother and brothers when all they ever did was cause me pain? Because I was the one hiding all of my true self. I had to go through the forgiveness process with my family or be stuck with the anger, rage, and resentment forever.

I learned my mother never really understood why I pulled away from her. She had no conscious recollection that my father abused me, drank alcohol, or that there was ritualistic abuse. Imagine her surprise. It took me ten years to see her without totally breaking down all the boundaries I'd built up. I was so ashamed of the family and thought my husband would leave me if he really saw how "sick" my family was. However, I had to take that chance.

Going back to New York was the hardest thing I've ever done. Parts of me wanted to go see my father and just stare at him with bulging eyes. I wanted him to see me, and I wanted to see him just to transfer his sick stuff back to him. I wanted to show him that not only did I succeed where he failed, but I wasn't going to allow him to destroy my life.

I had to stop wanting my father to come back and be the father I'd always dreamed about as a child. To pursue this fantasy, I would call him and talk like a little girl over the phone. When I tried to tell him about my anger toward him, he would hang up on me. I had to make the decision to stop calling him and accept the truth—he was never going to be the father I wanted and needed. This helped me to stop looking for father figures in my life.

Although I had the chance to confront him, I declined to do so. When I spoke with him over the phone the few times I called, he denied everything and wouldn't change his version of the story. I realized if I confronted him, all I'd get were his false self, his lies, and much pain I didn't need. Therefore, I didn't even go to the street where he lives. Why give him power? I learned to accept the truth for what it was. I would never have a happy reunion with him. He would never love me.

My mother was better in some ways and worse in others. I learned my mother was very assertive and could protect herself. She was still my mother and wanted me to parent her, but I tried not to be too responsible. I had to stop myself from buying her a toilet seat because hers was cracked. Imagine my agony over this. At first, I fell right back into the codependent relationship with my mother—centering my trip around her schedule and plans.

My brothers were in bad shape, not wanting to know what really happened between my father and me. They didn't question me about why they weren't invited to my wedding. One brother had poor hygiene and smoked as much as my mother. He hadn't bathed for three days when we saw him. Since he was living with my father, I didn't pick him up at his home. It was sad; he kept asking me to buy him cigarettes. I couldn't do it. Even if he wanted to kill himself, I wouldn't enable him. I felt like the mean sister again, denying him what he needed.

My other brother was in the hospital. He is schizophrenic and will be sick for the rest of his life. He knows he's sick and asks me to pray for him. I feel a special bond to this brother and I don't even know why. Out of all my family members, he has the most depth and intuition. He gets delusional and paranoid at times but is a wonderful human being.

At Christmas this year, he sent me a little teddy bear in a cup that says, "Everybody needs love." I feel so bad he can't live life to the fullest because he would've made a wonderful husband and father. When I call him, he keeps asking if I'm pregnant and if he can talk to my husband. We both tell him we love him and we pray for him.

The pain I felt reconnecting to my family was excruciating and emotionally draining. However, it was necessary for me to feel the pain instead of denying it or pretending my family was dead. Now, I'm more able to understand and accept their limitations, illnesses, and lifestyle. There is no greater gift than to be humbled by the truth. I realized just how brave and courageous I'd been to leave the family to find a new life and a new home.

What I've been able to add to my life as a result of reconnecting is a greater awareness of my assets. I feel more alive and more understanding of the ebb and flow of life. I no longer need to control my emotions, but can let them wash over me like a big wave. Although I now look forward to talking with my family, I still need to set limits with them. I share my healthy life with them since they know so little about that part of life. I can show them the beauty and help my family by balancing out some of the overwhelming pain and suffering they often feel.

In our lives, the three main ingredients we need are heart, intellect, and courage. Also, we need to find where home is. I've found my home and my security deep inside myself. For years I tried to be a different person with a different history. Finally, I realized I succeeded because of my history, not in spite of it. For ten years, I had to protect myself. I got married without telling my family because I thought I'd never reconnect with them. Furthermore, I also didn't think I would or could reconnect with God. One thing I've learned is to believe anything is possible.

If your family is abusive, I urge you to set limits and restrict contact. You need to decide what's best for you.

I'm sharing this with you because it was necessary for me to go to the next level of my life. I always heard that I needed to go back to New York to heal myself. I didn't know why but I needed to do this for my recovery.

A message I'd like to share is one that comes up repeatedly in my meditations. "The desire to make us over into love permeates the universe." This agrees with the other messages. We need to choose a path with our hearts if we are to ever be able to rise above hatred, violence, and prejudice—especially those feelings we have about ourselves. The more you love and accept yourself with your flaws and your strengths, the more you can move to a higher level of spiritual thinking. The more you realize you have the power within to choose your destiny, the more you can choose to no longer be a victim.

Spirituality, compassion, and forgiveness help us see the world in a better light. These concepts help me believe I'm needed as part of a larger plan to help the earth and other people. What is more exciting than unity and peace? How could I help others while holding in hatred, self-loathing, and depression from unresolved conflicts within my family?

By being honest about the truth, I was free to go forward. Even though I still have issues with depression, codependency, and abuse, I can acknowledge my imperfections and focus on my inner resources instead. I have to reinforce this choice one day at a time.

The following is a story that's very uplifting and empowering. It's about listening to our inner voice and is used as a hopeful scenario about our own inner resources. As you read the story, see if you can identify with any of the same feelings Potential had. Some questions follow the chapter to help you begin to locate your inner voice.

Shelter in the Forest

Once upon a time there was a girl named Potential. She had a habit of staying in her head and refusing to deal with any of her emotions. She analyzed everything and was afraid to try anything new because she thought people would laugh at her. She avoided all conflict and didn't believe in a power greater than herself. Potential was totally independent, claiming she didn't need help with anything. She lived alone and as she read romance novels would fantasize about how her life could be. She devoted her life to her job and believed her career would provide her with self-esteem.

On her way home from work one day, three people grabbed her, put a sheet over her head, and drove her to a dark forest. The captors told her she could escape by finding her way out of the forest. They took her watch and quickly ran away, leaving her alone and scared.

Potential wandered around in the dark until she came upon a house. She crept around until she saw a light from the kitchen. There were the three kidnappers sitting around the table talking loudly and laughing. As she listened at the door she realized these people were laughing at her.

The kidnappers had names printed on the backs of their shirts. They were named Shame, Fear, and Criticism. "Potential will never find her way out of this forest," Shame said shaking his head. "She's a flawed and defective human being." Shame continued by saying that Potential "was a mistake" and was afraid of telling anyone the truth about what happened. Fear agreed, saying Potential was too scared to succeed and leave the forest.

He went on to say, "She'll be lost forever. She's a scaredy cat and can't do it. She'll fail as she always does."

Criticism laughed along with the other two, saying, "Potential is stupid for even trying to find her way home. She never does anything right."

She didn't understand why they thought she would fail. She continued to listen until Fear whispered to the other two, "Let's hope she doesn't find Intuition and leave here." The others nodded their heads in agreement. "Intuition is her only hope of getting out of our trap," they said.

At this moment Potential felt the anger from deep inside her gut. She ran into the room, looked Fear right in the face, and said, "You three can't stop me! I'll find Intuition and she'll help me get home." Now Potential was connecting with her anger. "How dare you say those lies about me!" She ran out the door with a burst of energy she'd never felt before. She ran until she could run no more.

For days, she ran searching for Intuition until she was so hungry and frightened she started to think she might die in the forest and never find her way out. She was afraid Fear, Shame, and Criticism were right about her. "Maybe I am a misfit. Maybe I am a failure," she thought.

A voice deep inside her told Potential to slow down and pray. She had never prayed before but something told her to do it. "Please God," Potential prayed, "help me get home."

Like a gentle tap on the shoulder, she heard a small voice speak to her. The voice gave her direction and hope. She came upon a clearing and was almost blinded by a magnificent gold and white light in front of her. Soon she was face to face with Intuition. Intuition was beautiful with small, fine features. She exuded a sense of peace. Intuition said, "I knew you'd find me. Welcome home!"

"What do you mean, welcome home?" Potential shouted out of frustration, "This isn't my home." However, when she looked at Intuition she saw so much beauty and light. She was overwhelmed and touched by how at home she was feeling. She stepped back and began to see the rainbow in back of Intuition and a clear path home.

Intuition said, "You knew the way all along, Potential, but you just didn't believe in yourself. Go forth and believe in your own abilities. Face Fear and realize the power is within you to reach all of your goals. If you use me, Potential, you can walk in the light and succeed like you never believed possible." Finally, Intuition said, "I knew you would find me and leave Shame, Fear, and Criticism behind."

"What if they try to find me again and come after me?" Potential asked. "How can I stay far away from their influence?"

"Believe in the white and gold light that is always around you," Intuition replied. "Visualize my light, as I will always protect you from any negative influences. Together we are indestructible!" Lastly, Intuition told her, "Go spread the word to everyone you know to believe in a power greater than themselves and trust their intuition or inner voice."

Now Potential could call on her higher power and Intuition whenever negative thoughts crept into her mind. Potential left the forest with a renewed sense of purpose, ready to use her reserves to face the challenges ahead.

Shelter in the Forest—Discussion

In a crisis, we have inner resources to tap into. We have these tools inside us to not only deal with the situation, but to grow and change as a result. We can look at a crisis in one of two ways—we can focus on the fear or we can focus on the opportunity to grow and know ourselves better.

Potential found her way out of the forest by locating her inner resources. We can do the same. Intuition is defined as an inner knowing but we don't know how we know. Intuition is a storehouse of information we can use in our decision making. Fear, shame, and criticism undermine our ability to trust ourselves and move closer to our potential as human beings. The philosopher Goethe said, "Trust yourself, and you will know how to live." This is the aim of the story.

Questions for Thought and Discussion

1. What do you relate to in the story?
2. Do you know if your self-talk is negative or positive?
3. What things do you usually say to yourself in a time of crisis or turmoil?
4. What is your view of Potential in this story? What was wrong in her life?
5. What do the concepts of intuition and spirituality mean to you?
6. Do you ever listen to your intuition? Why?
7. Do you ever consult your inner voice during decision making times?

8. Have you ever surrendered to an unseen power before? Describe the incident.
9. Would you have done what Potential did in her situation? Why?
10. Would you utilize your higher self, intuition, or higher power if shame, fear, or criticism came back to influence you? How would you call on a higher power? How would you know you received an answer?
11. Are you deserving of a guide inside you who loves you? Why?

9

Completing the Past: Freedom from Bondage

In our society, we often value others before ourselves. We learn codependent and enabling behavior. Out of a need to please others we do things we really don't want to do. Potential had to get quiet enough and desperate enough to pray. This happens the same way for many recovering people.

How many of us were, or are, stuck in relationships which undermine our confidence and self-love? How many of us do the same things to ourselves by repeatedly judging and beating ourselves up with our mistakes? The awakening process is a beautiful one, which aims for wholeness and self-love.

I ask clients to take 15 minutes a day for quiet time. Some try but tell me they think about their laundry list and all they have to do later. Relaxing means we are doing nothing and being lazy. There is no time for reflection and renewal. My philosophy is that real wealth is developed in silence and by listening to our inner voice.

The concept of a powerful voice has always intrigued me. The story of Potential and Intuition explains how, as men and women, we can work with our inner selves, who have wisdom and the inner knowledge we seek. Intuition is committed to Potential, much like God or the higher power is committed to us.

"Shelter in the Forest" teaches the concept of a higher self. Our higher self is connected to our higher power. Shame, Fear, and Criticism are what Susan Jeffers calls the voices of our chatterbox. In her book, *Feel the Fear and Do it Anyway,* she explains that the chatterbox is a repository for every negative thought a person has ever received from parents, friends, etc. We can listen to our chatterbox or we can listen to our higher self. I help others create a positive tape of higher self messages.

Have you ever told the negative messages in your head to go away? Have you ever gotten mad at the negatives that keep popping up? This is precisely what everyone can do.

Potential lived in her head. She intellectualized and rationalized everything, especially her emotions. Potential was driven by her negative emotions but didn't make this connection. She wasn't even aware her feelings were against her until she heard them and was able to get angry.

For many of us, anger is a sin or is seen as a terrible emotion. I tell my clients emotions are not good or bad—just emotions. If they were always told they were failures or were always criticized, those negative tapes would continue to play even in their adulthood. We need to get in touch with our inner child and change those messages. Our inner resources are kind, powerful, and loving—just like Intuition. Potential needed to understand Intuition was a friend and protector. She needed to be so down and in despair that she had no other recourse except to pray.

How many of us pray only when things go wrong? I believe people have a hard time communicating with God or a higher power when all is well. Potential knew intuitively she needed to pray. This is an example of turning our will and our life over to the care of God as we understand him (step 3). Potential had to admit she couldn't do it alone, that she needed God, and was powerless.

Potential had never dealt with conflict. Therefore, her relationships were probably shallow or superficial. She used work to gain self-esteem and had no sense of balance in her life. However, not having any conflicts gives one the illusion of having control. In some ways, it's an escape from reality. Living life is not like a romance novel. I've seen many clients who would rather live in a fantasy world than face a confrontation.

For Potential, learning to ask for help was essential to her recovery. Leaving the forest had meaning for her because it gave her hope for a new day. Intuition told Potential she would protect her and to go spread the word about Intuition to others. This is how the message of a 12-step program gets passed along to others. To embark on a 12-step journey, we need to face the shame, fear, and old critical tapes that are inside us.

We can learn to stop our self-defeating and negative thoughts. Try doing some positive affirmations in the mirror or speak into a tape recorder. Record your anger on tape or write it in a journal. Don't eat, stifle, or swallow your anger. Anger is a healthy emotion. Have a book in which you record only the positive things that happen to you each day. Take a spiritual development workshop, class, or retreat.

Completing the Past

The way to move on with life is to heal your inner child and complete the past. We'll never get rid of the past but we don't have to keep on repeating old patterns. We complete the past by dealing with our hurt, grief, sadness, and pain. We tell our story to others who are safe and can empathize and relate.

In his book, *Healing the Child Within,* Charles Whitfield reminds us that being aware of our feelings is important. People who learn to feel and express them have a distinct advantage in eventually living a successful and peaceful life.

Some people come to therapy and say their childhood was fine and nothing bad happened to them. However, a small inner voice directed them to come to a session, or my ad in the local community paper jumped out at them. For whatever reason, they've asked for help and should be commended. Some people, however, know exactly why they come to therapy and are prepared to show me proof and documentation of their abuse by a parent or parents. Whatever the reason, both types of people are in pain.

Every family has problems and every person goes through maturation and crisis points in their lives. Developmentally, marriage is a crisis point and so is the birth of a baby. Therefore, we have many opportunities to seek help. If you don't have the coping skills to deal with a crisis, therapy could help. All we may need to do is verbalize our feelings or learn new coping skills.

I propose we start treating ourselves like the survivors and strong people we are. Have you ever felt as if you got through something difficult but don't know how you did it? I have days and weeks like that. We get through those times because we're unaware of the vast power and strength we have inside helping us do the tasks.

There are many therapists who believe personality is fixed at a certain age, usually by age five. They will tell you that as adults, we don't really change much. I disagree with that philosophy. I believe with hard work, consistency, and proper support, we can change. We can turn anger and pain into purpose, power, and love by using their energy and by believing in our own inner power. Your personality can change by working the 12-step program. You can also have real feelings and real relationships.

My friends from the program are wonderful. Connection to a recovering community is the closest thing I've found resembling a healthy family. Of course, there may be some people who need therapy but aren't getting it. Try to understand those people too. Spiritual growth is a way to not only transcend barriers, it's the way we're transformed into loving, self-actualized people. Understanding that begins in the heart and spreads outward is unity.

In graduate school, I knew a man who was a recovering alcoholic. He told me true happiness comes when we climb to the top of our mountain of pain. On top of the mountain we'll see a sign that says, "I forgive you." It's signed "Love, Yourself." Ultimately, the person we most need to forgive for our transgressions is ourselves. I was responsible for most of the self-hate and self-defeating behavior toward myself. Having compassion and forgiving myself for my flaws and imperfections were the keys to raising my self-esteem.

Endings and New Beginnings

My mother taught me something long ago that I still remember. She taught me to keep trying to find my dreams. Mother never gave up, despite obstacles and pain. She would always say, "When one door closes, another door opens." I truly believe in this philosophy.

I visualize a picture in my mind daily. I'm on a beautiful beach in Hawaii, lounging in the sun that shines on me without burning. I'm content, happy, and protected. One-hundred-dollar bills are falling out of the sky. Some of the money falls into a box marked "charity." I don't seem to mind that some of the money is given away. I relax and feel gratitude for these gifts.

Besides this picture, I visualize myself signing books at Krochs and Brentanos. People are waiting in line for my book. I'm a writer and I have arrived. You guessed it, the book I'm signing is *The River Within*. I couldn't reach these goals until I could imagine them first. Creative visualization moves your mind to a place where you can actually see your dreams become reality. This is not a magic solution—I also must work to make these dreams come true.

When you hear my first visualization, you might think it's about money and greed. However, it is really about spirituality and the myths I'm trying to break. When I relax and feel God's warmth, I'm content. I was never taught to relax. In my work, I always pushed and prodded. I never trusted that good would come to me unless I exhausted myself and was too responsible.

In the second visualization, I'm earning passive income—like book royalties. I never believed I could have money without an enormous amount of sweat and toil. The visualization allows me not only to rest, but to have money and not be afraid or anxious about it. When my mother worked as a waitress, I would count out her change every night. I'd feel guilty for wanting more in my life so I restricted my own beliefs about prosperity and having enough money. I always thought there was a lack of money for me. This belief limited how much money I thought I deserved. What are your beliefs about relaxation, money, and worth?

My inner self and spirituality are waiting for me in that visualization. Whenever I relax and rest in the faith I have, good things happen. When we rest in God or our higher power, we experience miracles and a feeling that we are truly living. True spirituality is connecting to the part of yourself that is pure love and light. I need to tell you the light will not burn or harm you.

My personal and professional goals focus on becoming an authentic person who not only speaks from the heart, but who is compassionate, whole, and kind. The River Within can hold us, warm us, and help us realize our potential. When we harvest the fruit of living a spiritual life, we're able to share this message with others who don't feel happy, alive, or connected.

The gifts we possess are meant to be shared and valued. Try to visualize yourself resting in God's love and light. Create a picture in your mind of where you want to go and realize you need to do what it takes to reach this goal. Start imagining the King or Queen within you. Believe in your own goodness and remember you are good enough and you deserve love and happiness. You will experience a freedom and a serenity you've never known before. Believe in the power of The River Within and the King or Queen who reigns inside you. You'll always be guided with gentle and loving messages.

10
Balance and the Model of Treatment

Achieving a sense of balance is one of the hardest things to do in our busy society. So many people operate by the "all or nothing" philosophy, it's hard to think about finding a middle ground. Many of us haven't learned to look at different areas of our lives that need attention and care. Learning how to live a balanced, happy, and healthy life takes time but is possible.

One of the guest speakers at my class on eating disorders at a local community college was from Overeaters Anonymous (OA). A student in my class asked, "Does a 12-step program teach people to live a balanced life?" The speaker laughed and confirmed that almost everyone was trying to find the middle of the road. Another speaker who is a teacher and nutritionist stated that the 12-step program is the best stress-management tool she's ever seen.

When people start feeding their spiritual needs, the rest of their lives become easier. The spiritual side is neglected because our society doesn't value spirituality.

At one of my Toastmasters' club meetings, I was sharing information about my spiritual development workshops with a businessman. He thought my spiritual development workshops would not generate income. Since other church-sponsored events were free, he felt I couldn't expect payment for them.

Treatment Model for Recovery

There was no way I was going to figure out how God operated, so I created my own framework for recovering clients. I developed a model of treatment which points out the stages of recovery (see next page). In therapy, we hook up the intellect with the emotions. This process consists of three stages that lead to action, change and growth, and healing (1) Awareness (2) Acceptance—healing inner wounds, attitudes, and beliefs (3) Wholeness and self-esteem building. Clients can work on all levels at the same time. However, for discussion, it helps to focus on them as steps in a process.

Awareness and Individuation

Awareness is needed to begin spiritual development. Without awareness, no one is going to believe he or she has an addiction or comes from a dysfunctional family. John Bradshaw claims this is due to the family spell that permeates a dysfunctional system. The family spell operates by a fixed set of rules or codes. Breaking this spell is the first step to recovery. Remember, denial is unconscious, and we can't change anything unless we come to know and accept it first. Many people have loyalty to their family of origin or play a protector role in the family— covering for a parent or sibling.

MODEL OF TREATMENT (3 A's)

AWARENESS + ACCEPTANCE + ACTION = CHANGE AND GROWTH

AWARENESS	ACCEPTANCE	ACTION	CHANGE AND GROWTH
↓	↓	↓	↓
ATTITUDES	EMOTIONS	RISK	SELF-LOVE SPIRITUALITY
↓	↓		
THOUGHTS	SELF-ESTEEM		

1. AWARENESS: ISSUES INVOLVED

Breaking denial (unconscious)
* Identify self-defeating patterns /chatterbox thinking
Abuses used (work, food, sex, people)
Cognitive restructuring

2. ACCEPTANCE: ISSUES INVOLVED

INTUITION
TRUST SELF
Family of origin work
Pain / fear: Emotional upset
Release shame/guilt
Abandonment/fear of rejection
Anger/depression/sadness
Self-love vs. self-loathing

3. ACTION : ISSUES INVOLVED

SPIRITUALITY:
* INTEGRATION
Dealing with the unknown
Breaking isolation
Setting boundaries
Self-care
Separation-individuation

The individuation part of this model is finding out if a person wishes to keep the values that his or her family has operated by. It's up to each person to decide which ones to keep and which ones to discard. This is a tremendous struggle because most families don't give permission for members to develop a strong sense of self. Since this is a healthy and normal part of growing up, I urge clients to engage in this struggle. Many clients aren't aware of how resistant the family is to their taking this step until they try to set boundaries or limits with family members.

Until they take time to listen, many people have no idea what negative tapes are playing inside them. Recovery is the process of self-discovery. Often, negative tapes are all a person hears. Many people don't feel lovable. Many people are caretakers but don't know how to care about themselves. Numerous clients of mine are angry at their family of origin and about things that happened to them in their childhood.

How many people love themselves unconditionally? How many of us received unconditional love from our parents? People in therapy learn how to love themselves despite flaws and to accept all of them and all of others. Individuation is a natural and healthy struggle for our own identity. It is never too late to individuate.

Also, I tell my clients that there's enough for them. We usually operate with concrete, finite thoughts. However, the concept of abundance explains that there is enough success, love, money, and food for everyone. The scarcity model tells us we need to eat all the food today because there may not be enough tomorrow. We need to hoard our good fortune or not share it for fear we'll never have another chance to get it.

To change this view, internal work needs to be done. When the thought of scarcity comes up, another part of you can stress that there will be many future meals. This is a technique called cognitive restructuring. This technique is used to change a person's beliefs, attitudes, and thoughts. Identifying problems, concerns, and self-sabotaging behavior helps with the restructuring process.

I ask clients what they want to happen when therapy is over. Since they're not in therapy for life, we work on goal setting. Many clients tell me they want to be happy or they want to feel alive. During this phase of treatment, I urge my clients to hook up with a 12-step group.

Acceptance and Healing Inner Wounds

The second stage of recovery is working on acceptance. In my practice, the hardest areas to work on with recovering people are self-forgiveness and the need to protect their parents. Some clients smile when they're hurting and use masks to cover pain and grief. A well-known professional speaker from Texas told other professional speakers that audiences were filled with many people in pain. Our society makes it hard for people to talk about pain. In this stage of therapy, clients begin to not only express pain but begin to release and feel the pain. Often in family therapy, siblings live in the same house and never share their feelings with one another. When the pain surfaces, the healing can begin.

Those who are in recovery face their own self-loathing, anger, and other emotions. They learn to accept themselves and grieve over lost opportunities. Most importantly, they feel significant and believe their feelings and opinions matter. By this time in therapy, people become empowered and can express the shame, anger, and fears they had as a child but were never able to express. They buried these emotions deep inside and pretended they went away.

This second phase of the model is the most painful and the most freeing. Social workers call this the middle phase. In this phase, the relationship between the client and the therapist is very important. The client needs to feel safe and trust that the therapist knows the way to happiness and will be a guide for him or her.

Wholeness, Self-Esteem Building, and Action

The third part of the model is the most exciting. When people feel good enough about themselves, they start taking small risks. Action is essential to the therapy process. Spiritual growth can occur. If clients are using their intuition, trusting themselves and a power greater than themselves, integration occurs. When people integrate the concepts of therapy with their spiritual growth, wholeness is the gift they find. When they can accept all parts of themselves, and all of others, their lives fill up with goodness and happiness.

Clients begin to take better care of themselves, set good boundaries with others, and create a supportive environment where they can get their needs met. The balance wheel is the foundation for life. A new sense of self-worth accompanies these positive changes. This part of recovery is truly beautiful but it's not perfect. The model serves as a foundation for growth that builds on peoples' strengths, not weaknesses. As we journey to the core of ourselves, we run into shame.

This core is beautiful, but it's hard to heal the shame protecting the core. Since we are living with the belief we're shame-based (I am a mistake), many will be afraid to look underneath the shame to find the diamond inside.

Underneath the shame *is* a diamond, and therapy can help you turn shame inside out to reach your true self.

We can unmask the true self and live a life of authenticity and self-love. When we embark on a journey into ourselves, we deal with all the parts we wish we could disown or get rid of. Many recovering clients want to disown or split off the parts they associate with their parents' flaws. To find wholeness, we need to embrace those parts, help them grow, and not judge them. This takes a great deal of compassion and honesty. Even in the darkness or shame, there is nourishment, information, and beauty.

Choosing to locate the diamond inside and finding the true self is a gift and an honor. To be who we are without pretense is the greatest pleasure in the world. The Model of Therapy makes it possible for us to be happy, whole, and self-confident. Do you have one or two people in your life with whom you can be totally yourself without pretense? If you do, this is the joy that comes from working with the model. We get support from others who are honestly looking into themselves and from our own storehouse of wealth, strength, and love—The River Within.

In the appendixes you will find spiritual development exercises, charts that will help you better understand the spiritual process, and a variety of useful information. Now you can be a student of spiritual growth.

The exercises are for learning purposes only—they're not meant to be a consistent in-depth course on this subject.

Also included in the appendixes are words of wisdom and worksheets that took me many years to create and disseminate. If you do some of the worksheets and feel uncomfortable, stop the exercise. You may wish to continue at another time.

The spiritual development test was not designed to criticize or make you feel uncomfortable about yourself or your position in the world. Focus on the parts you're doing well and build on them. Focus on what works and don't forget to answer from your heart! I hope you enjoy the exercises and charts. I wish you love and joy on your journey and hope to meet you on the recovery road.

Appendix A: Spiritual Development-Definitions/Charts/Tips

Spiritual Development

A. Spirituality

1. To be spiritual we must LIVE our lives/Trust in ourselves.
2. We must not fear the responsibilities and the work appointed to us by the will of the higher power or God. Service work is EMPOWERING.
3. We must KNOW what we are doing. Stay conscious and out of DENIAL.
4. We must have UNITY in our life (Wholistic--accept all of you and all of others)
5. Have compassion for ourselves/others.
6. The higher power creates and doesn't destroy.
7. We must have faith and RENEW that faith.
8. Believe that a relationship with the higher power is possible and positive.

B. Spiritual Issues and Messages

1. Age old search: Why are we alive? What is the best way to live life? What is our purpose/meaning on earth? Everyone has a life purpose.

2. Discontent is our spirituality waiting to happen.Spirituality is part of self-esteem

3. Major blocks to spiritual growth are: fear, shame, guilt, criticism and mistrust.

4. Others can give you spiritual gifts. A spiritual awakening might be an insight, a new feeling, or a gradual change.

5. Believe in ABUNDANCE. A higher power loves you unconditionally.

6. Spiritual development is open to EVERYONE. God cannot get to you if your mind is filled with negative thinking and the voices of your ego.

C. Difference Between Spirituality and Religion

Religion: the organized practice of a particular set of beliefs

Spirituality: a way of living that recognizes certain values with respect to self, others, nature and whatever one considers to be beyond this world.One may be a spiritual person and not be affiliated with any organized religion.

THE TWELVE STEPS

1. We admitted we were powerless over ____________-that our lives had become unmanageable.

2. Came to believe that a power greater than ourselves could restore us to sanity.

3. Made a decision to turn our will and our lives over to the care of God as we understand him.

4. Made a searching and fearless MORAL inventory of ourselves.

5. Admitted to God, to ourselves, and to another human being the exact nature of our wrongs.

6. Were entirely ready to have God remove all these defects of character.

7. Humbly asked Him to remove our shortcomings.

8. Made a list of all persons we had harmed, and became willing to make amends to them all.

9. Made direct amends to such people wherever possible, except when to do so would injure them or others.

10. Continued to take personal inventory and when we were wrong promptly admitted it.

11. Sought through prayer and meditation to improve our conscious contact with God as we understood him, praying only for knowledge of his will for us and the power to carry it out.

12. Having had a spiritual awakening as a result of these steps, we tried to carry this message to ____________ and to practice these principles in all our affairs.

THE STEPS IN PERSPECTIVE

STEP 1. Laying the foundation.
2. Promise of hope.
3. Act of faith (we need God in our lives).
4. Increase our awareness of who we are (know ourselves).
5. Honesty/Reconciliation (courage to proceed).
6. Reminds us of our powerlessness.
7. Needs us to ask to remove shortcomings-strength.
8. Restoring relationships (penance).
9. Forgive self/others-resentments. Rebuild self-esteem.
10. What we are today-ABUNDANCE THINKING!
11. Faith and persistence.
12. Plan for those who wish to enter the realm of the spirit. SERVICE/COMMUNITY.

SPIRITUALITY: FROM SHAME BASED TO RESPECT BASED

SHAME BASED: Fear, self-pity, perfectionism, resentment, control, pride, and ego. Aim is self-destruction and all or nothing thinking. The focus is on lack and depressive thinking patterns.

RESPECT BASED: Trust, self-care, gratitude, self-acceptance, honesty, healthy shame, and guilt. A belief that the universe is supportive. The focus is on abundance and prosperity.

ADDICTION: Detachment from God. We don't need him. We can feel powerful and believe that we can remove the pain as well. Alcohol, drugs, food or people become our God. The only one we rely on is the one that eventually destroys us and those we love. The addict continues to believe he or she has power/control.

Steps to Serenity

HAPPINESS/SERENITY
SERVICE TO COMMUNITY
ACCEPT ALL OF YOU AND OTHERS
HEALTH/NUTRITION
ABUNDANCE THINKING! PROSPERITY
RISK SHARING YOUR TRUE SELF
TOOLS CAN BE USED-PRAY OR REACH OUT
MEDITATION/SOLITUDE/QUIET TIME DAILY
STEP GROUP/12-STEP GROUP TO HEAL ISOLATION
TRUST IN SELF/ HIGHER SELF/ INTUITION
BELIEF IN A POWER GREATER THAN YOURSELF
ADMIT POWERLESSNESS

ISSUES/CONCERNS THAT BLOCK SPIRITUAL GROWTH

1. We mistrust others and fear we won't "do it right."
2. We will disappoint/ not deserving of unconditional love.
3. We won't get what we ask for.

WAYS TO ENHANCE SPIRITUAL GROWTH/BREAK BARRIERS

1. Think POSITIVE thoughts daily/ affirmations/ fill up with the good.
2. Cultivate a "gratitude attitude". Focus on the doughnut, not the hole.
3. Believe that the higher power loves you just for being you.
4. Uncover and work on your co-dependent patterns.
5. Be open to connect to the higher power through 12-step groups or friends.
6. Ask for help. We can't do it alone, even if we think we can!
7. Believe in abundance- you will always be taken care of and have enough!
8. Face your fears. Take small risks in a safe place to grow and prosper.

SCARCITY (SHAME BASED)	VS.	ABUNDANCE (RESPECT BASED)
1. WORRY, DOUBT IN ONESELF (I never have enough, I always have bad luck!)		TRUST, FAITH IN ONESELF (I will have enough!) (I deserve good things!)
2. "CHATTERBOX" NEG. THINKING		"HIGHER SELF" POSITIVE THINKING
3. KNOWN RESULTS (Even if it is unhealthy)		UNKNOWN RESULTS RISKING NEW BEHAVIOR
4. "I CAN'T/I AM NOT GOOD ENOUGH THINKING"		"I AM GOOD" "I CAN DO IT!"

Tips for Creating Spiritual Growth and Development

1. Change old thoughts about God as an authority figure who is going to punish you. Realize and visualize that the higher power creates and doesn't destroy.

2. Have a symbol or an image for your higher power as you understand him or her. This can be a glowing ball, a beautiful woman, nature, etc.

3. Make quiet time a priority for yourself. Affirmations and prayers help daily.

4. Work a 12-step program. Spiritual development is open to everyone. God cannot get to you if your mind is filled with negative thoughts.

5. Remove blocks to spiritual development (fear, shame, guilt, and criticism).

6. Think of spiritual growth as a part of self-esteem and as a resource.

7. Service work can be done for the wrong reasons. If you don't enjoy helping others and don't feel empowered, it may not be the right path for you.

8. Believe the higher power loves you unconditionally. Just be yourself. You don't have "to do" anything.

9. Realize other people can give you spiritual gifts. A spiritual awakening might be an insight, a new feeling of joy, or a gradual change.

10. Focus on the fact that there is a meaning and a purpose for you. Everyone has a life purpose. What is your purpose on earth?

11. Believe God or the higher power will take you where you need to go if you let the process evolve. Trust in the process and remember you can't skip steps. Go with the flow.

Appendix B: Spiritual Development Exercises

Understanding the 12-step program for Recovering Clients

1. Why did you make the decision to buy this book?

____

____

____

____

2. We all have a purpose and a plan as human beings. Write a MISSION STATEMENT about your plan/purpose on earth. (You may or may not see your mission connected to your present career.)

MISSION STATEMENT____

____

____

3. Name three of your gifts or talents that you possess.(You have some whether you think so or not!)

____

____

____

BELIEFS ABOUT SPIRITUALITY

SPIRITUALITY...

I can look inward and feel peaceful.
Spirituality is a part of self-esteem.
I'm afraid of spirituality.

GOD...

God loves me.
I'm afraid of God.
I'm undeserving of God's love.

MY LIFESTYLE....

I'm grateful for my quiet time.
I don't know what my life purpose is.
Living for me means merely surviving.

Now think of all the things these words mean to you.

1.Spirituality______________________________________
____
2. God____
____
3. My lifestyle_____________________________________
____

Answer the following questions:-

1. Where did these beliefs come from?________________
____
2. What beliefs do I want to adopt?__________________
____
3. What spiritual misconceptions do I have?____________
____

1. SPIRITUAL JOURNEY

A. Pick a turning point in your life. Address the following questions:

1. When did it occur?
2. What was the turning point?
3. What wisdom came out of this experience?
4. How did you respond that might have been different from another person in the same situation

B. Decisions are often based on what is known and what is intuitively felt. Write down one of your positive spiritual experiences. Was your intuition right? Do you make decisions based on your intuition in the present? Why or why not?

SPIRITUAL DEVELOPMENT

0	*1*	*2*	*3*	*4*	*5*	*6*	*7*	*8*	*9*	*10*
never			sometimes			often				always

1. __ Do you forget to think about what you are grateful for?"
2. __ Do you get down on yourself for making mistakes?
3. __ Do you magnify your problems and view the world with suspicion?
4. __ Do you tend to wear a mask so others won't see your shortcomings?
5. __ Do you have a hard time accepting all of you and all of others?
6. __ Do you have negative and critical self-talk on a daily basis?
7. __ Do you tend to hold on to anger and resentment?
8. __ Do you sometimes not care if you hurt anyone (this includes yourself!)
9. __ On a daily basis, are you out of touch with your real feelings?
10. __ Do you live on a treadmill, using action as distraction?
11. __ Do you isolate yourself if you are feeling vulnerable, scared, or depressed?
12. __ Do you have a hard time integrating achievements and the goodness in you?
13. __ Do you tend to procrastinate and sabotage your success?
14. __ Do you feel negative about your life and live in either the past or future?
15. __ Are you afraid to turn your life over to a power greater than yourself because you fear that power will hurt or punish you?

TOTAL _____

Score

Below 95: OUTSTANDING-You have a positive, spiritual nature that is secure inside of you. You have a great sense of intuition.

106-96: EXCELLENT-You have trust and faith in the higher power as well as yourself! Continue to develop your higher self or intuition.

107-117: GOOD-You have the knowledge. Now you need to put it into action. Continue to work on the steps with relationship issues.

128-118: FAIR- Stop taking back control, and believe in yourself and the concept of a loving higher power. Go back to steps 1 through 3.

139-129: POOR-You need to get a sponsor, read more, or study spiritual writings to understand this positive process! Don't give up. All you need is some trust and guidance.

150-140: You are displaying many ACOA and codependent traits. You need to turn inward. Perhaps a 12-step or treatment group would help you! You need a WAKE-UP call!

BELIEFS ABOUT SPIRITUALITY SHAPE OUR LIVES

Spiritual myths and misconceptions:

1.

2.

3.

4.

5.

What I now accept as truth:

1.

2.

3.

4.

5.

These beliefs need to be reinforced and thought about often. One must be committed to spiritual growth on a daily basis and also be willing to work on obstacles and blocks to spirituality.

My goal for spiritual growth is ____________________________
by ____________________________ 19__

signed ____

EXERCISE: Write a letter to yourself and tell yourself what goals or what things you will do this year to increase your awareness and spiritual growth. You can sign it with your name or a part of yourself that is helping you (example: signed, your intuitive self, or your smart self, or your spiritual self, etc)

Appendix C: Spiritual Development Material and Information

STEPS TO SPIRITUAL GROWTH-HOW TO HAVE AN INNER LIFE

CODEPENDENCY (outer life)	SPIRITUALITY (inner life)
SHAME BASED	EXPOSING, EMBRACING FEELINGS/ RESPECT BASED
ALL OR NOTHING THOUGHT DISTORTIONS	TURN WILL AND LIFE OVER FAITH IN HIGHER POWER
CONTROL	WE HAVE NO CONTROL
SELF-ESTEEM COMES FROM APPROVAL SEEKING/ EXTERNAL PROVING	TRUST IN YOURSELF "TAKE WHAT YOU WANT AND LEAVE THE REST"
CARETAKING/ PEOPLE PLEASING GIVE TO GET	BELIEF THAT YOU ARE LOVABLE/ TAKE CARE OF INNER CHILD
ADDICTIONS/ MOOD ALTER FEELINGS	ALLOW THE FEELINGS TO SURFACE.
ISOLATION/ FEAR OF GROUPS	SELF-ACCEPTANCE 12- STEP GROUP
LACK OF BOUNDARIES	SAFETY/SET LIMITS SELF-PROTECTION
TREADMILL ACTIVITY "ACTION IS DISTRACTION"	QUIET TIME/ MEDITATION/PRAYER INTEGRATION
SPIRITUAL BANKRUPTCY	SPIRITUAL GROWTH AND AWARENESS

CONCEPT OF WHOLENESS - THE STRESS WHEEL

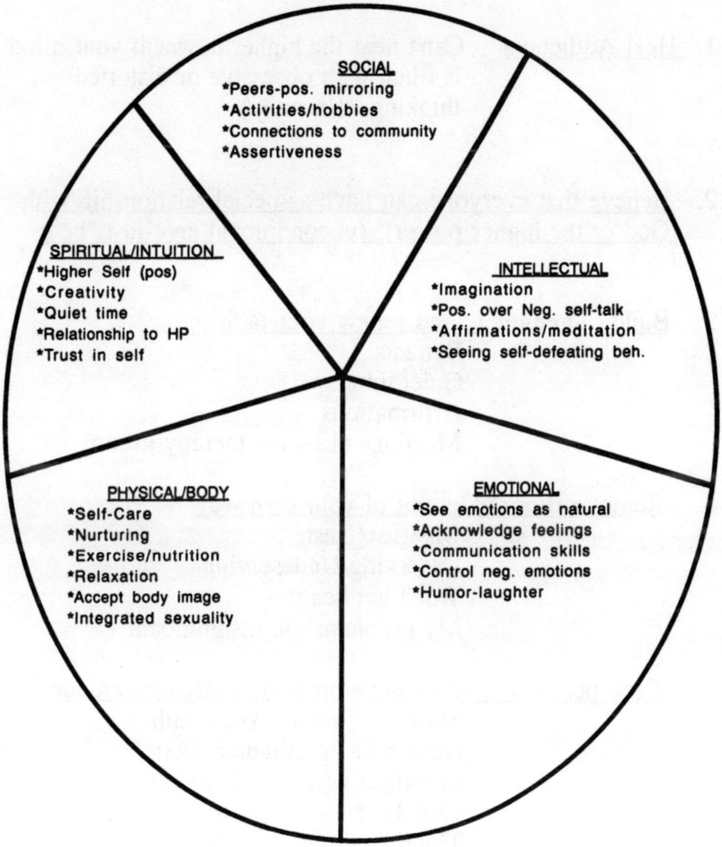

Spiritual Development

1. Heal Addictions : Can't hear the higher power if your mind is filled with obsessive or distorted thinking. (Insanity)

2. Believe that everyone can have a special relationship with God or the higher power! (unconditional love-just "be")

3. Build , strengthen, and renew your faith
   - Retreats
   - Quiet time
   - Affirmations
   - Meetings (12-step, therapy group)

4. Remove Blocks-Get out of your own way
   - Mistrust/Trust
   - Deserving/Undeserving
   - Won't get heard
   - My problems are insignificant

5. Each person's spiritual development is different/unique
   - Solitude/ Practice your faith
   - Develop a "gratitude attitude"
   - Self-discovery
   - Face Fear
   - Think positive
   - Change codependent patterns

RECOVERY ISSUES

Grieving for past and current issues

Difficulty being real

Neglecting our own needs

Self-loathing/meaninglessness in our lives

Fear of abandonment

Over Responsible/control issues

Lack of boundaries/lack of self-esteem building

Increased tolerance for inappropriate behavior

Difficulties with trust, love, feelings, and assertiveness

Guilt, shame, all or nothing thinking

Respect and authority issues

Negative self-talk

Mis-perception of others' feelings, motives, and behavior

ADDICTION VS. RECOVERY

COMPULSION	→	COMPASSION
"DOING"	→	"BEING"
SELF-CENTERED (EGO ORIENTED)	→	SOCIAL RESPONSIBILITY
LIES/DRIVEN (PERFORMANCE)	→	TRUTH SERENITY
UNEQUAL/IMMATURE	→	MATURE
POWER/SUPERIORITY	→	FREEDOM
VIOLENCE/BLAME	→	PERSONAL RESPONSIBILITY
SELF-HATRED HOSTILE/SPLITTING	→	SOLITUDE ACCEPTANCE
CODEPENDENCY (Outer Life/Otheration)	→	SPIRITUALITY (Inner Life/Purpose)
SELF AS GOD GRANDIOSITY	→	HIGHER POWER HIGHER SELF/INTUITION

The Building Blocks of Serenity:

FAITH	PEACE
Honor inner voice	History is not destiny
Give/Receive	No victims/only choices
Remove Blocks	To "be" vs. To "do"
Abundance thinking	Living your dreams

Remember: We can't skip steps

Don't push it

Don't think discontent is a negative feeling

Use your faith/serenity like a resource

YOU hold the key that opens the door to serenity

" The key to serenity: When you know and believe without question or doubt that in all you do, God is there to help you out."

BIBLIOGRAPHY

Alcoholics Anonymous. *Twelve Steps and Twelve Traditions*. New York: Alcoholics Anonymous World Services, Inc., 1981 Edition.

Beattie, Melody. *Codependent No More*. Minnesota: Hazelton, 1987.

Bly, Robert. *A Little Book on the Human Shadow*. San Francisco: Harper, 1988.

Bradshaw, John. *The Family*. Florida: Health Communications, Inc., 1988.

____. *Home Coming*. New York: Bantam Books, 1990.

____. *Healing the Shame That Binds You*. Florida: Health Communications, 1988.

Erikson, Erik H. *Childhood and Society*. New York: WW Norton & Co., 1963.

Fox, Matthew. *A Spirituality Named Compassion*. New York: Harper & Row, 1979

Jeffers, Susan. *Feel the Fear and Do it Anyway*. New York: Fawcett Columbine Books, 1987.

Hay, Louise. *You Can Heal Your Life*. California: Hay House, Inc., 1984.

Hazelton Foundation. *The Twelve Steps of Alcoholics Anonymous*. New York: Harper & Row Publishers, Inc., 1974.

____. *Stairway to Serenity: The Eleventh Step.* Minnesota: Hazelton, 1988.

Keating, Thomas. *The Heart of the World.* New York: Crossroad, 1989.

Klass, Joe. *The 12 Steps To Happiness.* New York: Ballantine Books, 1982.

Larson, Earnie. *Stage II Recovery.* San Francisco: Harper & Row, 1985.

Martin, John A. *Blessed Are The Addicts.* San Francisco: Harper Collins Publishers, 1990.

Merton, Thomas. *Thoughts In Solitude.* New York: The Noonday Press, 1956.

Middelton-Moz, Jane. *Shame and Guilt.* Florida: Health Communications, 1990.

Paulson, Pat A., Brown, Sharon C., and Wolf, Jo Ann. *Living on Purpose.* New York: Fireside Books, 1988.

Recovery Publications. *The 12 Steps: A Way Out Working Guide.* San Diego: Recovery Publications Inc., 1989 Revised Edition.

Roger, John and McWilliams, Peter. *You Can't Afford the Luxury of a Negative Thought.* Los Angeles: Prelude Press, 1988.

Vaughan, Frances E. *Awakening Intuition.* New York: Anchor Press, 1979.

____. *The Inward Arc.* Boston: Shambhala Publications Inc., 1985.

Whitfield, Dr. Charles L. *Healing The Child Within.* Florida: Health Communications, 1987.

Give the Gift of Empowerment to Your Friends and Colleagues!

= *ORDER FORM* =

***YES**, I want ___ copies of The River Within* at $12.95 each, plus $3 shipping per book. (Illinois residents please include $1.00 sales tax per book.) Canadian orders must be accompanied by a postal money order in U.S. funds. Allow 30 days for delivery.

___ **YES**, I am interested in having Karen Schultz speak or conduct a workshop for my organization, school, or group. Please send information. Audiences are energized and empowered by Karen's guidance on how to locate and tap into The River Within, your own storehouse of power, strength, and inner wisdom.

Name ______________________ Phone ________________

Organization ____

Address ____

City/State/Zip ______________________________________

Please make your check payable and return to:

Inner Space Publishing
900 Jorie Blvd., Suite 234
Oak Brook, IL 60521

or call

(708) 352-6587